Anonymous

The Druggists' Reference Book

1892: consisting of various and useful information arranged in tabulated

form, selected from Lindsay & Blakiston's physician's visiting list

Anonymous

The Druggists' Reference Book
*1892: consisting of various and useful information arranged in tabulated form,
selected from Lindsay & Blakiston's physician's visiting list*

ISBN/EAN: 9783337869960

Printed in Europe, USA, Canada, Australia, Japan

Cover: Foto ©Andreas Hilbeck / pixelio.de

More available books at **www.hansebooks.com**

THE

DRUGGISTS' REFERENCE BOOK

1892,

consisting of various and useful information, arranged in tabulated form, selected from

LINDSAY & BLAKISTON'S

PHYSICIAN'S VISITING LIST,

and including a very

COMPLETE DOSE TABLE

of the official and unofficial Drugs, according to the English and Metric Systems, arranged in accordance with the

U. S. PHARMACOPŒIA, 1890,

which is preparing for publication, and in which the metric system has been adopted.

☞ SEE SPECIAL OFFER BELOW.

PRICE LIST.

THE PHYSICIAN'S
VISITING LIST, 1892.

(Lindsay & Blakiston's.)

Forty-first Year of its Publication.

— — · · —

REGULAR EDITION.

For 25 Patients per day or week.	Gilt Edges, pencil, pocket, etc.,						$1.00
50 " " " "	" " " "						1.25
75 " " " "	" " " "						1.50
100 " " " "	" " " "						2.00
50 " " " 2 Vols. { Jan. to June / July to Dec. }							2.50
100 " " " 2 Vols. { Jan. to June / July to Dec. }							3 00

INTERLEAVED EDITION.

For 25 Patients per day or week. Gilt Edges, pencil, pocket, etc.,	$1.25
50 " " " " " " "	1.50
100 " " " " 2 Vols. { Jan. to June / July to Dec. }	3.00

PERPETUAL EDITION.

Same as the regular edition, but without Dates, and with Special Memorandum Pages. Can be commenced at any time and used until full. Bound in handsome red leather. Gilt edges.

For 1300 names, interleaved, tucks, pocket and pencil, ... $1.25
2600 " " " " " 1 50

MONTHLY EDITION.

Name of patient need be written but once during the month, the whole month's account being kept in one place. Can be commenced at any time.

Leather cover, pocket, pencil, gilt edges, with tucks, ... $1.00
" " " " " " without tucks, ...75

EXTRA Pencils will be sent, postpaid, for 25 cents per half dozen.

"For completeness, compactness, and simplicity of arrangement, it is excelled by none in the market."—*New York Medical Record.*

— — — —

SPECIAL OFFER TO DRUGGISTS.

This **Physician's Visiting List** is not only sold by many wholesale and retail Druggists, but by not a few it is given as a **Christmas** or **New Year's Present** to those physicians who use their store or reside in the same town or neighborhood.

To those druggists using it in this way, we furnish the book with the Physician's name stamped on in Gilt Letters, compliments of, etc., at *special prices.*

May be ordered through your Wholesale Druggist or Bookseller.

CONTENTS.

CALENDAR FOR 1892.

JANUARY.

S	M	T	W	T	F	S
					1	2
3	4	5	6	7	8	9
10	11	12	13	14	15	16
17	18	19	20	21	22	23
24	25	26	27	28	29	30
31						

FEBRUARY.

S	M	T	W	T	F	S
	1	2	3	4	5	6
7	8	9	10	11	12	13
14	15	16	17	18	19	20
21	22	23	24	25	26	27
28	29					

MARCH.

S	M	T	W	T	F	S
		1	2	3	4	5
6	7	8	9	10	11	12
13	14	15	16	17	18	19
20	21	22	23	24	25	26
27	28	29	30	31		

APRIL.

S	M	T	W	T	F	S
					1	2
3	4	5	6	7	8	9
10	11	12	13	14	15	16
17	18	19	20	21	22	23
24	25	26	27	28	29	30

MAY.

S	M	T	W	T	F	S
1	2	3	4	5	6	7
8	9	10	11	12	13	14
15	16	17	18	19	20	21
22	23	24	25	26	27	28
29	30	31				

JUNE.

S	M	T	W	T	F	S
			1	2	3	4
5	6	7	8	9	10	11
12	13	14	15	16	17	18
19	20	21	22	23	24	25
26	27	28	29	30		

JULY.

S	M	T	W	T	F	S
					1	2
3	4	5	6	7	8	9
10	11	12	13	14	15	16
17	18	19	20	21	22	23
24	25	26	27	28	29	30
31						

AUGUST.

S	M	T	W	T	F	S
	1	2	3	4	5	6
7	8	9	10	11	12	13
14	15	16	17	18	19	20
21	22	23	24	25	26	27
28	29	30	31			

SEPTEMBER

S	M	T	W	T	F	S
				1	2	3
4	5	6	7	8	9	10
11	12	13	14	15	16	17
18	19	20	21	22	23	24
25	26	27	28	29	30	

OCTOBER.

S	M	T	W	T	F	S
						1
2	3	4	5	6	7	8
9	10	11	12	13	14	15
16	17	18	19	20	21	22
23	24	25	26	27	28	29
30	31					

NOVEMBER.

S	M	T	W	T	F	S
		1	2	3	4	5
6	7	8	9	10	11	12
13	14	15	16	17	18	19
20	21	22	23	24	25	26
27	28	29	30			

DECEMBER.

S	M	T	W	T	F	S
				1	2	3
4	5	6	7	8	9	10
11	12	13	14	15	16	17
18	19	20	21	22	23	24
25	26	27	28	29	30	31

THE

METRIC OR FRENCH DECIMAL SYSTEM OF WEIGHTS AND MEASURES.

BY

OSCAR OLDBERG, Pharm. D.

The metric system is based upon the METER, which is the standard unit of *length* of that system, and equal to 39.370432 inches, or about 10 per cent. longer than the yard.

The metric unit of *fluid measure* is the LITER — the cube of $\frac{1}{10}$ Meter, or 1000 Cubic-centimeters — equal to about 34 fluid ounces.

The metric unit of *weight* is the GRAM, which represents the weight of one Cubic-centimeter of water at its maximum density. It is equal to about 15 grains.

One CUBIC-CENTIMETER is equal to about 16 minims.

IN WRITING PRESCRIPTIONS IT IS SUFFICIENTLY ACCURATE AND SAFE TO CONSIDER 1 GRAM AS EXACTLY EQUAL TO 15 TROY GRAINS, AND TO CONSIDER 1 CUBIC-CENTIMETER AS EQUAL TO 15 MINIMS.

We accordingly have:—

> 1 Gram equal to 15 troy grains.
> 1 troy grain equal to $\frac{1}{15}$ Gram.
> 1 Cubic-centimeter equal to $\frac{1}{4}$ fluid drachm.
> 1 fluid drachm equal to $\frac{1}{4}$ Cubic-centimeter.

Hence—

1. TO CONVERT TROY GRAINS INTO GRAMS, OR MINIMS INTO CUBIC-CENTIMETERS:—

a. *Divide by 10, and from the quotient subtract one-third;* or, b. *Divide by 15;* and

2. TO CONVERT APOTHECARIES' DRACHMS INTO GRAMS, OR FLUID DRACHMS INTO CUBIC-CENTIMETERS, *multiply by 4.*

In writing prescriptions the "Gram" (abbreviated "Gm.") and "Cubic-centimeter" (abbreviated "C. c.," which may be called "fluigram," and written "f Gm") only, should be used.

All other terms, and units, and prefixes, used in the metric system, may be wholly ignored by the physician and the pharmacist.

Example of a Metric Prescription.

> ℞. Hydrarg. Chloridi. Corros.....................0 25 Gm.
> Potassii Iodidi .... 10 00 Gm.
> Aquæ...100 00 C. c.
> Tinct. Cinch. Comp.. ....100,00 C. c.
> Mix.

The use of a decimal line prevents possible errors.

To write a prescription for fifteen doses of any medicine, write it first for *one* dose in *grains* and *minims*, and then substitute the same number of "Grams" and "fluigrams," thus:—

> ℞. Opii............................gr. i.
> Camphoræ ....gr. i j.
> Make one pill,

and to get fifteen such doses in metric terms, write:—

> ℞. Opii........................... 1 Gm.
> Camphoræ .... 2 Gm.
> Make fifteen pills.

The Gram and the Cubic-centimeter (*fluigram*) when referring to liquids, may be considered as equal quantities, except the liquids be very heavy (as in the case of chloroform) or very light (as in the case of ether).

Measures may be discarded and weights exclusively employed, if preferred. All quantities in a prescription would then be expressed in GRAMS.

The average "DROP" (water) may be considered equal to 0.05 C. c., or 0.05 *Gm.* An average TEASPOON holds 5 C. c., and an average TABLESPOON 20 C. c. Decimal numbers should be used as far as practicable without sacrifice of accuracy as to strength and dose of the preparation. It is safe to prescribe 30 *Gm.* for one troy ounce, and 250 C. c. for eight fluid ounces.

TABLE FOR CONVERTING APOTHECARIES' WEIGHTS AND MEASURES INTO GRAMS.

TROY WEIGHT. Grains.	METRIC. Grams.	APOTHECARIES' MEASURE.	GRAMS FOR LIQUIDS. Lighter * than Water.	Specific Gravity † of Water.	Heavier ‡ than Water.
1/60	.00016	℥ 1	.055	.06	.08
1/80	.00033	2	.10	.12	.15
1/24	.0005	3	.16	.18	.24
1/60	.00065	4	.22	.21	.32
1/8	.001	5	.24	.30	.40
1/40	.0015	6	.32	.36	.48
1/30	.002	7	.38	.42	.55
1/20	.003	8	.45	.50	.65
1/16	.004	9	.50	.55	.73
1/12	.005	10	.55	.60	.80
1/10	.006	15	.80	.72	.96
1/8	.008	16	.90	1.00	1.32
1/6	.010	20	1.12	1.25	1.60
1/4	.016	25	1.40	1.55	2.00
1/3	.02	30	1.70	1.90	2.50
1/2	.03	35	2.00	2.20	2.90
1	.065	40	2.25	2.50	3.30
2	.13	48	2.70	3.00	4.00
3	.20	50	2.80	3.12	4.15
4	.26	60 f℥j	3.40	3.75	5.00
5	.32	72	4.00	4.50	6.00
6	.39	80	4.50	5.00	6.65
8	.52	90	5.10	5.60	7.50
10	.65	96	5.40	6.00	8.00
15	1.00	100	5.60	6.25	8.30
20 Ɔj	1.30	120 f℥ij	6.75	7.50	10.00
21	1.50	160	9.00	10.00	13.30
26	1.62	180 f℥iij	10.10	11.25	15.00
30 ℈ss	1.95	240 f℥ss	13.50	15.00	20.00
40	2.60	f℥v	16.90	18.75	25.00
50	3.20	f℥vj	20.25	22.50	30.00
60 ℈j	3.90	f℥vij	23.60	26.25	35.00
120 ℈ij	7.80	f℥j	27.00	30.00	40.00
180	11.65	f℥ij	51.00	60.00	80.00
210 ℈ss	15.50	f℥iij	81.00	90.00	120.00
300	19.10	f℥iv	108.00	120.00	160.00
360	23.30	f℥v	135.00	150.00	200.00
420	27.20	f℥vi	162.00	180.00	240.00
480 ℥j	31.10	f℥viij	216.00	240.00	320.00

* Lighter than water are tinctures, spirits, compound spirit of ether, sweet spirit of nitre, fixed and volatile oils. Æther Fortior, f℥j = grams 2.80.

† Same as water are waters, liquids, decoctions, infusions, most fluid extracts, and t'nctures made with dilute alcohol

‡ Heavier than water are syrups, glycerin, a few fluid extracts, and chloroform Of the latter, f℥j = grams 5.50.

3

POSOLOGICAL TABLE

(Meadow's).

The following Posological Table is taken from the Guy's Hospital Pharmacopœia. It is to be read as follows: Suppose that the maximum dose of a given liquid is one fluid ounce, the dose for an infant one month old is thirty minims. If the substance be a solid, and the maximum dose is sixty grains, then the dose for an infant of a month old is three grains, and so on for the several ages stated. The maximum doses are given at the top of each of the three columns, and the doses for the different ages are opposite to those ages.

Age.	Maximum Dose.		
	One fluid ounce.	Twenty grains.	Sixty grains.
One month.............................	minims 30	gr. 1	grs. 3
Three months.......................	——	——	grs. 4
Six months.............................	minims 40	grs. 2	grs. 6
Nine months...........................	——	——	grs. 7
One year..............................	fl. dr. j.	grs. 3	grs. 8
Two years.............................	fl. drs. iss.	grs. 4	grs. 10
Three years...........................	fl. drs. iss.	grs. 4	grs. 12
Four years............................	fl. drs. ij.	grs. 5	grs. 15
Five years............................	fl. drs. ijss.	grs. 6	grs. 18
Six years.............................	fl. drs. iij.	grs. 7	grs. 20
Seven years..........................	fl. drs. iijss.	grs. 8	grs. 25
Eight years...........................	fl. oz. ss.	grs. 10	grs. 30
Ten years.............................	fl. drs. ivss.	grs. 12	grs 35
Twelve years.........................	fl drs. v.	grs. 14	grs 40
Thirteen years.......................	fl. drs. vss.	grs 15	——
Fifteen years........................	fl. drs. vj.	grs. 16	grs. 45
Eighteen years.......................	fl. drs. vjss.	grs. 17	——
Twenty years.........................	fl. drs. vij.	grs. 18	grs. 50
Twenty to forty-five years........	fl. oz. j.	grs. 20	grs. 60
Fifty years...........................	fl. drs. vij.	grs. 18	grs. 50
Sixty to seventy years..............	fl. drs. vj.	grs 16	grs. 45
Eighty to ninety years..............	fl. drs. v.	grs. 14	grs. 40
One hundred years...................	fl. oz. ss.	grs. 10	grs. 30

DOSE TABLE.

GIVING THE DOSES OF OFFICIAL AND UNOFFICIAL DRUGS
IN BOTH THE ENGLISH AND METRIC SYSTEMS.

COMPILED SPECIALLY FOR THE PHYSICIAN'S VISITING LIST.

FOR 1892.

THOROUGHLY REVISED AND CORRECTED BY GEORGE M. GOULD, M.D.,
OPHTHALMIC SURGEON TO THE PHILADELPHIA HOSPITAL;
AUTHOR OF "A NEW MEDICAL DICTIONARY," ETC.

The Doses given are for adults; for children the following rule
(Young's) will be found the most convenient. Add 12 to the age, and divide by the age, to get the denominator of the fraction, the numerator of
which is 1. Thus, for a child two years old, $\frac{2+12}{2} = 7$ and the dose is one-
seventh of that for an adult. Of powerful narcotics scarcely more than
one-half of this proportion should be used. Of mild cathartics, two or even
three times the proportion may be employed.

In a general way it may be said that approximately the dose for a child
of one month is $\frac{1}{20}$ that of an adult; for one of 3 months, $\frac{1}{15}$; 6 months, $\frac{1}{10}$;
1 year, $\frac{1}{8}$: 2 years, $\frac{1}{6}$; 3 years, $\frac{1}{5}$; 5 years, $\frac{3}{10}$; 8 years, $\frac{1}{4}$; 10 years, $\frac{3}{8}$; 12
years, $\frac{1}{2}$; 15 years, $\frac{2}{3}$; 20 to 45 years, adult dosage; 50 years, $\frac{5}{6}$; 60 years, $\frac{3}{4}$;
80 years, $\frac{2}{3}$.

For Hypodermatic Injection, the dose should be one-half of that
used by the mouth; by rectum, five-fourths of the same.

The letters gr. stand for grains; ℥, minims; ♌, drachms; ℥, ounces; gm.,
grams; cgm., centigrams.

REMEDIES.	DOSE. APOTH.	DOSE. METRIC.	REMEDIES.	DOSE. APOTH.	DOSE. METRIC.
Abstract.			Acid. gallic.,	gr. 3–15	0.200–1.000
aconiti, . .	gr. ¼–½	0.016–0.033	gall. in albu-		
aspidosperm	" 5–20	0.333–1.333	minuria,	" 10–60	0.666–4.000
belladonnæ, .	" ½–1½	0.033–0.100	hydrobrom.		
cannab. ind.	" 1–3	0.066–0.200	3i ♀. . .	" 10–15	0.666–1.000
conii, . .	" 1–2	0.066–0.133	hydrobrom.		
digitalis, .	" 1–3	0.066–0.200	dil., . .	♌ 40–52	2.666–8.000
gelsemii, .	" 1–3	0.066–0.200	hydrochlor,	" 3 10	0.200–0.666
hyoscyami,	" 2–5	0.133–0.333	hydrochlor.		
iguatiæ, .	" 1–3	0.066–0.200	dil., . .	" 10–30	0.666–2.000
ipecac, . .	" 3–30	0.200–2.000	hydrocyan.		
jalapæ. . .	" 6–10	0.400–0.666	dil., . .	" 2 6	0.133–0.400
nuc. vom., .	" ¼ 1₃	0.016–0.033	lactic, . .	gr. 15–60	1.000–4.000
phytolaceæ,	" 5 15	0.333–1.000	nitr, . .	♌ 3 10	0.200–0.666
pilocarpi, .	" 6–30	0.400–2.000	nitr. dil., .	" 10–30	0.666–2.000
podophylli,	" 4–10	0.266–0.666	nitro-hydro-		
senegæ, .	" 4–10	0.266–0.666	chlor, .	" 3–10	0.200–0.666
valerianæ,	" 10–15	0.666–1.000	nitro-hydro-		
veratr. vir.,	" 1–3	0.066–0.200	chlor. dil.,	" 5–20	0.333–1.333
Acet. lobeliæ,	♌ 15–30	1.000–2.000	phosphoric		
opii, . . .	" 5 16	0.333–1.066	(50%), .	gr. 3–15	0.200–1.000
sanguinar,	" 15–30	1.000–2.000	phosphoric		
scillæ, . .	" 10 30	0.666–2.000	dil., . .	♌ 10–30	0.666–2.000
Acid. acet. dil.	" 60–90	4.000–6.000	salicylic, .	gr. 5–20	0.333–1.333
arsenios, .	gr. ¼–⅒	0.001–0.003	sulphuric, .	♌ 5–10	0.333–0.666
benzoic, .	" 5 15	0.333–1.000	sulph. dil.,	" 5–30	0.333–2.000
boric, . .	" 5–10	0.333–0.666	sulphuric		
carbolic,	" 1–3	0.066–0.200	arom., .	" 5–10	0.333–0.666

Remedies.	Dose. Apoth.	Dose. Metric.
Acid. sulphur.	♏ 30-30	2.000-4.000
tannic, . .	gr. 2-10	0.133-0.666
Aconit. (white crystals),	" 1/400-1/200	0.000167-0.0003
Adonidin, . .	" 1/16-1/10	0.004-0.006
Aloe, ...	" 2-5	0.133-0.333
Aloinum, . .	" 1-3	0.066-0.200
Alumen, . .	" 10-15	0.665-1.000
Ammonii benzoas, . .	" 10-20	0.666-1.333
bromid, . .	" 5-30	0.333-2.000
carb. . . .	" 3-10	0.2000-0.666
chlorid, . .	" 10-30	0.666-2.000
iodid, . .	" 3-15	0.200-1.000
phosph, . .	" 5-20	0.333-1.333
picras, . .	" 1/4-1/2	0.016-0.033
sulph, . .	" 3-15	0.200-1.000
valer, . .	" 3-15	0.200-1.000
Amyl nitris, .	♏ 2-5	0.133-0.333
Amylum iodatum, . .	gr. 3-30	0.200-2.000
Antifebrin, .	" 2-15	0.133-1.000
Antimonii et pot. tartr.; diaph, .	" 1/20-1/12	0.003-0.005
et pot. tartr.; emetic, .	" 1-2	0.066-0.133
oxid, . . .	" 1½-2	0.100-0.133
oxysulphur.	" ½-2	0.033-0.133
sulphid, .	" ½-2	0.033-0.133
sulphuret, .	" ½-2	0.033-0.133
Antipyrin, .	" 10-20	0.666-1.333
Apiol, . . .	" 3-5	0.200-0.333
Apomorph. hydrochlor,	" 1/30-1/10	0.002-0.006
Aqua ammon.	♏ 6-30	0.400-2.000
amygd. amar	ʒ 2-4	8.000-16.000
camphoræ,	℥ ½-2	16.000-64.000
chlori, . .	ʒ 1-4	4.000-16.000
creasoti, .	" 1-4	4.000-16.000
laurocerasi,	♏ 6-30	0.400-2.000
Argenti iodid.	gr. ½-2	0.033-0.133
nitras, . .	" 1/6-1/3	0.011-0.022
oxid, . . .	" ½-2	0.033-0.133
Arsenii iodid.	" 1/64-1/10	0.001-0.006
Assafœtida, .	" 5-20	0.333-1.333
Atropina, . .	" 1/128-1/32	0.0005-0.002
Atropinæ sulp.	" 1/128-1/32	0.0005-0.002
Auri et sodii chlorid, .	" 1/32-1/16	0.002-0.004
Bebcerinæ sul.	" 3-10	0.200-0.666
Berberina, and its salts, .	" 3-15	0.200-1.000
Bismuthi citr.,	" 3-15	0.200-1.000
et ammon. citr., . .	" 1-15	0.066-1.000
subcarb, .	" 6-30	0.400-2.000
subnitr, . .	" 30-60	2.000-4.000
tannas, . .	" 6-30	0.400-2.000
valer, . .	" 1-3	0.066-0.200
Brayera, . .	ʒ 2-6	8.000-24.000
Brucina, . .	gr. 1/64-1/13	0.001-0.004
Caffeina, . .	" 1-5	0.066-0.333
Caffeinæ citras	" 1-5	0.066-0.333
Calcii bromid.,	" 5-30	0.333-2.000
carb. . . .	" 15-60	1.000-4.000
hypophosph.	" 3-15	0.200-1.000
iodidum, .	" 1-3	0.066-0.200
Calcii phosph.	" 15-30	1.000-2.000
Calx sulphur.,	" 1/3-1	0.022-0.066

Remedies.	Dose. Apoth.	Dose. Metric.
Camphora, .	gr. 3-10	0.200-0.666
Camph. monob.	" 2-5	0.133-0.333
Cantharis, .	" ½-2	0.033-0.133
Capsicum, .	" 1-3	0.066-0.200
Castoreum, .	" 6-15	0.400-1.000
Catechu, . .	" 15-30	1.000-2.000
Cerii nitras, .	" 1-3	0.066-0.200
oxalas, . .	" 1-3	0.066-0.200
Chinoidinum,	" 3-30	0.200-2.000
Chloral, . .	" 3-20	0.200-1.333
Chloroformum	♏ 1-5	0.066-0.333
Chrysarobin,	gr. 3-15	0.200-1.000
Cinchona, . .	" 15-60	1.000-4.000
Cinchonidina, and its salts	" 1-30	0.066-2.000
Cinchonina, and its salts	" 1-30	0.066-2.000
Cinnamomum,	" 6-30	0.400-2.000
Cocaine sol. p.c.	1-4	
Codeina, . .	gr. ½-2	0.033-0.133
Confectio sen.,	" 1-2	0.066-0.133
Coniina, and its salts, . .	" 1/64-1/32	0.001-0.002
Copaiba, . .	♏ 15-60	1.000-4.000
Cota, . . .	gr. 1-2	0.066-0.133
Cotoina, . .	" 1/6-½	0.011-0.033
Creasotum, .	♏ 1-3	0.066-0.200
Creta præpar,	gr. 15-75	1.000-5.000
Croton chloral,	" 1-5	0.066-0.333
Cubeba, . .	" 15-60	1.000-4.000
Cupri acetas,	" 1/16-1/4	0.004-0.016
sulphas, .	" 1/4-1/2	0.016-0.033
Cupri am., .	" 1/6-1	0.011-0.066
Curare, . .	" 1/32-1/6	0.002-0.011
Curarina, . .	" 1/64-1/20	0.001-0.003
Daturine, . .	" 1/100-1/50	0.00067-0.00134
Decoct. aloes comp., .	℥ ½-2	16.000-64.000
sarsap. comp.	" 2-6	64.000-192.000
Digitalinum,	gr. 1/64-1/32	0.001-0.002
Digitalis, . .	" ½-2	0.033-0.133
Duboisina, and its salts, .	" 1/128-1/60	0.0005-0.001
Elaterinum; U.S.P. 1880,	" 1/60-1/13	0.001-0.005
Elaterium; U.S.P. 1870	" 1/10-1/6	0.0066-0.011
Emetina, and salts, emet.	" 1/8-1/4	0.008-0.016
and salts, diaph, .	" 1/120-1/30	0.0005-0.002
Emulsio hydrocyan, .	ʒ ½-1	2.000-4.000
Ergota, . .	gr. 15-60	1.000-4.000
Ergotinum, .	" 2-8	0.133-0.533
Eserina, and its salts, .	" 1/64-1/20	0.001-0.003
Extr. absinthii	" 2-6	0.133-0.400
absinth. fluid	♏ 15-30	1.000-2.000
achilleæ, .	gr. 3-10	0.2000-0.666
achilleæ fluid	♏ 15-60	1.000-4.000
aconiti fol. (Engl.), .	gr. 1/3-½	0.022-0.033
aconiti fol.; U.S.P. 1870,	" 1/3-½	0.022-0.033
aconiti fol. fluid, . .	♏ 1-5	0.066-0.333
aconiti rad.; U.S.P. 1880	gr. 1/12-1/4	0.005-0.015

REMEDIES.	DOSE. APOTH.	DOSE. METRIC.
Extr. aconiti [rad] fluid	♏ ⅓- 2½	0.033-0.166
aletridis fl.,	" 15-30	1.000-2.000
alni rub. fl.,	" 15-30	1.000-2.000
aloes aquos.	gr. ½- 3	0.033-0.200
alston const. fl., . . .	ʒ 1- 4	4.000-16.000
angelicæ rad fl., . . .	♏ 30-60	2.000-4.000
angusturæ fl	" 15-45	1.000-3.000
anthemidis,	gr. 2-10	0.133-0.666
anthemidis fl	♏ 30-60	2.000-4.000
apocyni andros fl., .	" 8-50	0.533-3.333
apocyni cannab. fl., .	" 8-30	0.533-2.000
araliæ hisp. fl., . . .	" 30-60	2.000-4.000
araliæ nudic. fl., . . .	" 30-60	2.000-4.000
araliæ racem fl., . . .	" 30-60	2.000-4.000
araliæ spin fl., . . .	" 30-60	2.000-4.000
arecæ fl., .	" 45-75	3.000-5.000
arnicæ flor.,	gr. 3- 8	0.200-0.533
arnicæ fl., .	♏ 5-15	0.333-1.000
arnicæ rad.,	gr. 2- 5	0.133-0.333
arnicæ rad. fl	♏ 5-15	0.333-1.000
aromat. fl.,	" 30-60	2.000-4.000
ari triphylli fl., . . .	" 15-30	1.000-2.000
asari fl., .	" 15-30	1.000-2.000
asclep. incar. fl., . . .	" 15-30	1.000-2.000
asclep. syr. fl	" 15-30	1.000-2.000
asclep. tuber. fl., . . .	" 15-30	1.000-2.000
aspidii fl., .	ʒ 1- 4	4.000-16.000
aspidosperm. fl., . . .	♏ 15-45	1.000-3.000
aurantii cort fl., . . .	ʒ ¼- 2½	1.000-10.000
azedarach fl.,	♏ 15-75	1.000-5.000
baptisiæ fl.,	" 7-30	0.465-2.000
bellad. alcohol, . .	gr. ⅙-½	0.011-0.033
bellad. fol, (Engl.), .	" ⅙-⅔	0.011-0.044
bellad. fol. fl.	♏ 3- 6	0.200-0.400
bellad. rad.,	gr. ⅛- ¼	0.008-0.016
bellad rad. fl	♏ 1- 3	0.066-0.200
berber aqui fol. fl., .	" 15-30	1.000-2.000
berber. vulg. fl., . . .	" 15-30	1.000-2.000
boldi fl., .	" 3-15	0.200-1.000
brayeræ fl,	ʒ 2- 4	8.000-16.000
bryoniæ fl.,	♏ 15-60	1.000-4.000
buchu fl., .	ʒ ½- 2½	2.000-10.000
calami fl., .	♏ 15-60	1.000-4.000
calend. fl., .	" 15-60	1.000-4.000
calumbæ, .	gr. 3-10	0.200-0.666
calumbæ fl.,	♏ 15-60	1.000-4.000
canellæ fl.,	" 15-60	1.000-4.000
cannab. Am. fl., . . .	" 3-15	0.200-1.000
cannab ind.,	gr. ⅙-½	0.011-0.033
cannab. ind. fl., . . .	♏ 3- 6	0.200-0.400
capsici fl., .	" 1- 3	0.066-0.200
Extr. cardam comp. fl.,	♏ 15-45	1.000-3.000
cardui ben. fl.	" 15-60	1.000-4.000
carnis, . .	gr. 15-60	1.000-4.000
cascara sag-rad. fl., .	♏ 10-20	0.666-1.333
cascarillæ fl.	ʒ ¾- 2½	3.000-10.000
castaneæ fl.,	" ¾- 2½	3.000-10.000
catariæ fl.,	" ¼- 1¼	1.000-5.000
catechu liq.,	♏ 8-30	0.533-2.000
caulophylli fl	" 15-30	1.000-2.000
chelidonii fl.	" 15-30	1.000-2.000
chelonis fl.,	" 30-60	2.000-4.000
chimaph. fl.,	ʒ ¾- 1¼	3.000-5.000
chionanthi fl	" ¾- 2½	3.000-10.000
chirettæ fl.,	" ½- 1¼	2.000-5.000
cimicifugæ fl	♏ 8-30	0.533-2.000
cinchoniæ,	gr. 15-30	1.000-2.000
cinchoniæ fl.	♏ 30-60	2.000-4.000
cinchoniæ arom. fl.,	" 30-60	2.000-4.000
cinchoniæ comp. fl.,	ʒ ½- 1¼	2.000-5.000
cocculi fl., .	♏ 1- 3	0.066-0.200
colch. rad.,	gr ⅓- 1½	0.022-0.100
colch rad. fl.	♏ 2- 4	0.133-0.266
colch. sem. fl.	" 1½- 6	0.100-0.400
collinsoniæ fl	" 30-60	2.000-4.000
colocynth, .	gr. 1½- 5	0.100-0.333
colocynth comp., .	" 1½- 5	0.100-0.333
condurango fl., . . .	♏ 8-30	0.533-2.000
conii fol. (Engl.). .	gr. 1- 4	0.066-0.266
conii fol. alc.; U.S.P.1870	" 1- 1½	0.066-0.100
con. [fr.] alc.; U.S.P.1880	" ⅓- 1	0.022-0.066
conii fol. fl.,	♏ 1- 2	0.066-0.133
con. [fr.] fl.; U S.P.1880	" 1½- 5	0.100-0.333
convallariæ rad. fl. .	" 15-30	1.000-2.000
coptidis fl.,	" 30-60	2.000-4.000
corn. flor. fl.,	" 30-60	2.000-4.000
corydalis fl.,	" 15-30	1.000-2.000
coto fl., . .	" 3-15	0.200-1.000
cubebæ fl., .	" 15-30	1.000-2.000
cypripedii fl.	" 15-60	1.000-4.000
damianæ fl.,	ʒ ½- 2½	2.000-10.000
delphinii fl.,	♏ 1- 3	0.066-0.200
digitalis, .	gr. ⅙- ½	0.011-0.033
digitalis fl,	♏ 1- 6	0.066-0.400
dioscoreæ fl,	" 15-30	1.000-2.000
ditæ fl., . .	ʒ 1- 4	4.000-16.000
dracontii fl.	gr. 30-60	2.000-4.000
droseræ fl.,	♏ 5-10	0.333-0.666
dulcamaræ,	gr. 5-15	0.333-1.000
dulcamaræ fl	ʒ 1- 2	4.000-8.000
ergotæ, . .	gr. 1½- 8	0.100-0.533
ergotæ fl., .	♏ 15-60	1.000-4.000
eryodictyi fl.	" 15-30	1.000-2.000
erythroxyli fl., . . .	ʒ ½- 2	2.000-8.000
eucalypti fl.,	♏ 15-60	1.000-4.000
euonymi fl.,	" 15-60	1.000-4.000
eupatorii fl.,	" 30-60	2.000-4.000
euphorb. ipec. fl., .	" 5-30	0.333-2.000
ferri pom.,	gr. 3-15	0.200-1.000

Remedies.	Dose. Apoth.	Dose. Metric.	Remedies.	Dose. Apoth.	Dose. Metric.
Extr. frangulæ fl.,	ʒ ½-2½	2.000-10.000	Extr. lycopi fl.	♏ 5-30	0.333-2.000
frankeniæ fl.	♏ 8-15	0.533-1.000	malti,	ʒ 1-2½	4.000-10.000
gallæ fl.,	ʒ ¾-2	3.000-8.000	manzanitæ fl	" ½-2	2.000-8.000
gelsemii,	♏ 2-8	0.133-0.533	marrubii fl.,	" 1-2	4.000-8.000
gelsemii fl.,	" 5-20	0.333-1.333	matico fl.,	♏ 30-60	2.000-4.000
gent. fl.,	" 30-60	2.000-4.000	matricariæ,	" 8-30	0.533-2.000
gent. com. fl.	" 30-60	2.000-4.000	menisperm. fl	" 30-60	2.000-4.000
gent. quin. fl.	" 15-30	1.000-2.000	methystice fl	" 15-60	1.000-4.000
geranii fl.,	" 15-30	1.000-2.000	mezerei,	gr. ½-1	0.033-0.066
gei fl.,	" 15-30	1.000-2.000	mezerei fl.,	♏ 3-10	0.200-0.666
gilleniæ fl.,	" 15-30	1.000-2.000	micromeriæ,	" 15-60	1.000-4.000
gossypii fl.,	" 15-45	1.000-3.000	mitchellæ fl.	" 30-60	2.000-4.000
granati rad. cort. fl.,	ʒ ¾-2	3.000-8.000	myricæ fl.,	" 30-60	2.000-4.000
grind. rob. fl.	♏ 30-60	2.000-4.000	nectandræ,	ʒ 1-4	4.000-16.000
grind. squar. fl.,	" 30-60	2.000-4.000	nuc. vom.,	gr. ⅛-½	0.008-0.033
guaiaci ligni fl.,	" 30-60	2.000-4.000	nuc. vom. fl.,	♏ 1-5	0.066-0.333
guaranæ fl.,	" 15-30	1.000-2.000	nuphar fl.,	" 5-15	0.333-1.000
hæmatoxyli,	gr. 8-30	0.533-2.000	nymphææ fl.	" 5-15	0.333-1.000
hæmatoxyli fl.,	♏ 30-60	2.000-4.000	œnotheræ fl.,	" 15-30	1.000-2.000
hamamelid. fl.,	" 30-90	2.000-6.000	opii,	gr. ⅙-½	0.011-0.033
helleb. nigris	gr. ½-3	0.033-0.200	papaveris,	" ½-2	0.033-0.133
helleb. nigris fl.,	♏ 5-15	0.333-1.000	papaveris fl.,	♏ 15-45	1.000-3.000
heloniæ fl.,	" 8-30	0.533-2.000	pareiræ fl.,	" 30-60	2.000-4.000
hepaticæ fl.,	" 30-60	2.000-4.000	petroselina fl	ʒ 1-2	4.000-8.000
humuli,	gr. 3-15	0.200-1.000	phellandrii fl	" 1-2	4.000-8.000
humuli fl.,	♏ 30-60	2.000-4.000	phoradend. fl.	" ½-1	2.000-4.000
hydrangeæ fl	" 30-60	2.000-4.000	physostigmæ	gr. 1/16-⅙	0.004-0.011
hydrastis,	gr. 3-10	0.200-0.666	physostigmæ fl.,	♏ 1-3	0.066-0.200
hydrastis fl.,	♏ 8-30	0.533-2.000	phytolaccæ baccar. fl.,	" 5-30	0.333-2.000
hyoscyami (Engl.),	gr. 1-4	0.066-0.266	phytolaccæ rad.,	gr. 1-3	0.066-0.200
hyoscyami alc.,	" 1-2	0.066-0.133	phytolaccæ rad. fl.,	♏ 5-30	0.333-2.000
hyoscyami fol. fl.,	♏ 3-15	0.200-1.000	pilocarpi fl.,	" 15-60	1.000-4.000
hyoscyami sem. fl.,	" 2-8	0.133-0.533	pimentæ fl.,	" 15-45	1.000-3.000
ignatiæ,	gr. ¼-½	0.016-0.033	piper. nigr. fl	" 15-45	1.000-3.000
ignatiæ fl.,	♏ 1-6	0.066-0.400	piscidiæ fl.,	" 15-60	1.000-4.000
ipecac fl.,	" 3-60	0.200-4.000	podophylli,	gr. ½-1½	0.033-0.100
iridis versic.	gr. 3-6	0.200-0.400	podophylli fl.	♏ 8-30	0.533-2.000
irid. versic. fl	♏ 15-30	1.000-2.000	polygoni fl.,	" 15-30	1.000-2.000
jaborandi fl.,	" 10-60	0.666-4.000	polygonati fl.	" 5-15	0.333-1.000
jalapæ; U.S. P. 1870,	gr. 5-10	0.333-0.666	populi fl.,	" 30-60	2.000-4.000
jalapæ alc.,	" 3-6	0.200-0.400	prinos fl.,	" 30-60	2.000-4.000
jalapæ fl.,	♏ 15-30	1.000-2.000	prun. virg. fl.	" 30-60	2.000-4.000
juglandis,	gr. 15-30	1.000-2.000	pteleæ,	" 15-30	1.000-2.000
juglandis fl.,	ʒ ¾-2	3.000-8.000	pulsatillæ fl.	" 2-5	0.133-0.333
junip. fl.,	♏ 30-60	2.000-4.000	quassiæ,	gr. 1-5	0.066-0.333
kamala fl.,	" 30-60	2.000-4.000	quassiæ fl.,	♏ 30-60	2.000-4.000
kino, liquid,	" 15-30	1.000-2.000	quercus fl.,	" 30-60	2.000-4.000
krameriæ,	gr. 5-15	0.333-1.000	rhamni cath. ft. fl.,	" 30-60	2.000-4.000
krameriæ fl.	♏ 30-60	2.000-4.000	rhamni purs. cort. fl.,	" 30-120	2.000-8.000
lactucæ,	gr. 5-15	0.333-1.000	rhei,	gr. 5-15	0.333-1.000
lactucæ fl.,	♏ 15-60	1.000-4.000	rhei fl.,	♏ 15-45	1.000-3.000
lactucarii fl.,	" 8-30	0.533-2.000	rhus arom. fl	" 15-60	1.000-4.000
lappæ fl.,	ʒ 1-2	4.000-8.000	rhus glabr. cort. fl.,	" 30-60	2.000-4.000
laricis fl.,	" ½-2	2.000-8.000	rhus glabr. fruct. fl.,	" 30-60	2.000-4.000
leonuri fl.,	♏ 30-60	2.000-4.000	rhus toxicod. fl.,	" 1-6	0.066-0.400
leptandræ,	gr. 3-10	0.200-0.666	ricini fol. fl.,	ʒ ½-2	2.000-8.000
leptandræ fl.	♏ 30-60	2.000-4.000	rosæ fl.,	" ½-2	2.000-8.000
lobeliæ fl.,	" 1-5	0.066-0.333	rubi fl.,	♏ 15-60	1.000-4.000
lupulini fl.,	" 5-15	0.333-1.000	rumicis fl.,	" 30-60	2.000-4.000
			rutæ fl.,	" 15-30	1.000-2.000
			sabbatiæ fl.,	" 30-60	2.000-4.000
			sabinæ fl.,	" 5-15	0.333-1.000

REMEDIES.	DOSE. APOTH.	DOSE. METRIC.
Extr. salicis fl.	ʒ ½- 2	2.000-8.000
salviæ fl., .	" ½- 2	2.000-8.000
sambuci fl.,	" ½- 2	2.000-8.000
sanguin fl.,	♏ 5-15	0.333-1.000
santali citr. fl	ʒ 1- 2	4.000-8.000
santonicæ fl.	♏ 15-60	1.000-4.000
sarsap. fl., .	ʒ ½- 2	2.000-8.000
sarsap. comp. fl., ...	" ½ 2	2.000-8.000
sassafras fl.,	" ½- 2	2.000-8.000
scillæ fl., .	♏ 5-30	0.333-2.000
scillæ comp fl., ...	" 5-30	0.333-2.000
scoparii fl.,	ʒ ½ 1	2.000-4.000
scutellariæ fl	" ½- 2	2.000-8.000
senecionis fl.	" 1- 2	4.000-8.000
senegæ fl., .	♏ 8-15	0.533-1.000
sennæ fl., .	ʒ 1- 4	4.000-16.000
serpent. fl.,	♏ 30-60	2.000-4.000
simarubæ fl.,	" 15-30	1.000-2.000
solidag. fl.,	" 30-60	2.000-4.000
spigeliæ fl.,	" 15-60	1.000-4.000
spigeliæ et sennæ fl.,	ʒ ½- 2	2.000-8.000
stillingiæ fl.,	" ½- 2	2.000-8.000
stillingiæ comp. fl.,	" ½- 2	2.000-8.000
stramonii (Engl.), .	gr. ½- 1	0.033-0.066
stramonii fol. alc , .	" ⅓ ⅔	0.022-0.044
stramonii sem., . . .	" ⅙ ½	0.011-0.033
stramonii fl.,	♏ 1- 6	0.066-0.400
sumbul fl., .	" 15-60	1.000-4.000
taraxaci, .	gr. 5-15	0.333-1.000
taraxaci fl.,	ʒ ½- 2	2.000-8.000
thujæ fl., .	♏ 8-15	0.533-1.000
toxicodendri fl., ...	" 1- 5	0.066-0.333
trifol prat. fl	ʒ 1- 2	4.000 8.000
trillii fl., .	" ½ 2	2.000-8.000
trit. rep. fl.,	" 1- 4	4.000-16.000
tussilag. fl.,	♏ 30-60	2.000-4.000
urticæ rad fl	" 5-15	0.333-1.000
ustilag. maid fl., ...	" 15-60	1.000-4.000
uvæ ursi fl ,	" 30-60	2.000-4.000
vaccin. crassifol. fl., .	" 30-60	2.000-4.000
valerian, .	gr. 5-15	0.333-1.000
valer. fl., .	♏ 30-60	2.000-4.000
veratr vir. fl	" 2- 8	0.133-0.533
verbenæ,	" 15-60	1.000-4.000
viburni opuli fl., . . .	ʒ 1- 2	4.000-8.000
viburni [prunifol.] fl.,	" 1- 2	4.000-8.000
wahoo, . .	gr. 1- 5	0.066-0.333
xanthoxyli cort, fl., .	♏ 15-30	1.000-2.000
xanthoxyli fruct. fl.,	" 15-30	1.000-2.000
zingiberis fl .	" 8-30	0.533-2.000
Fel bovis purif.	gr. 3- 6	0.200-0.400
Ferri arsen, .	" 1/20-½	0.003-0.033
benzoas, .	" 1- 5	0.066-0.333
bromid, . .	" 1- 5	0.066-0.333
carb. sacch.,	" 4 15	0.267-1.000
chlorid, . .	" 1- 3	0.066-0.200
citr, . , .	" 5-10	0.333-0.666
Ferri et ammon. citr.,	gr. 5-10	0.333-0.666
et ammon. sulph., .	" 5-10	0.333-0.666
et ammon. tartr, .	" 5-15	0.333-1.000
et cinchonid. citr., . .	" 5-10	0.333-0.666
et pot. tartr.,	" 15-60	1.000-4.000
et quin citr.	" 5-10	0.333-0.666
et strych. citr	" 1- 5	0.066-0.333
hypophosph. .	" 5-10	0.333-0.666
iodidum, .	" 1- 5	0.066-0.333
iodidum sac.	" 2- 3	0.133-0.200
lactas, . .	" 1- 3	0.066-0.200
oxalas, . ,	" 1- 3	0.066-0.200
oxid. magnet	" 5-10	0.333-0.066
oxid. hydrat,	℥ ½- 2	16.000-64.000
phosphas, .	gr. 1- 5	0.066-0.333
pyrophosph.	" 1- 5	0.066-0.333
subcarb, .	" 5-30	0.333-2.000
sulphas, .	" 1 3	0.066-0.200
sulph. exsic.	" ½- 1½	0.033-0.100
valer, . .	" 1- 3	0.066-0.200
Ferrum dialys,	♏ 1-15	0.066 1.000
reduct, . .	gr. 1- 5	0.066-0.333
Gamboge, . .	" 1- 4	0.066-0.267
Gaultheria, oil of, . . .	♏ 3-10	0.200-0.666
Guarana, . .	gr. 8-30	0.533-2.000
Hydrarg. chlo. corros., .	" 1/64-1/10	0.001-0.006
chlorid. mite	" ⅙- 8	0.011-0.533
iodid. flav.,	" ⅙- 1	0.011-0.066
iodid. rubr.,	" 1/50 1/10	0.0013-0.006
iodid. vir.,	" ⅙- 1	0.011-0.066
subsulp flav.	" ¼-½	0.016-0.033
c. creta, . .	" 3- 8	0.200-0.533
Hydrastin, .	" 5-10	0.333-0.666
Hyoscine, . .	" 1/100-1/70	0.00067-0.001
Hyoscyamina and salts,	" 1/128-1/32	0.0005-0.002
Hypnone, . .	♏ 5-10	0.033-0.066
Ichthyol, . .	gr. 3- 4	0.200-0.266
Infusum bray.	℥ 2- 8	64.000-256.000
digitalis, .	ʒ 2- 4	8.000-16.000
sennæ comp	℥ 1- 2	32.000 64.000
Iodoformum,	gr. 1- 3	0.066-0.200
Iodol, . . .	" ⅙-½	0.011-0.033
Ipecacuanha, expect., . .	" ⅙- 1	0.011-0.066
emetic, . .	" 15-30	1.000-2.000
Jalapa, . .	" 15-30	1.000 2.000
Kairine, . .	" 3-30	0.200-2.000
Kamala, . .	ʒ 1- 2	4.000-8.000
Kino, . . .	gr. 8 30	0.533 2.000
Lactucarium,	" 8-15	0.533 1.000
Lewinin p.c. sol	50 p. c.	
Liq. ammon. acet., . .	ʒ 2- 8	8.000-32.000
acidi arseni.	♏ 2- 7	0.133-0.467
arsen. et hydr. iod.,	" 2- 7	0.133 0.467
ferri chloridi	" 2-10	0.133-0.666
ferri dialys,	" 1-15	0.066-1.000
ferri nitrat,	" 8-15	0.533 1.000
pepsini, . .	ʒ 2- 4	8.000-16.000
Liquor potassæ	♏ 5-30	0.333-2.000
potas. arsen.	" 3- 7	0.200-0.467
potas. citrat.	ʒ 2- 4	8.000-16.000

Remedies.	Dose. Apoth.	Dose. Metric.
Liquor sodæ,	♏ 5-30	0.333-2.000
sodii arsen.,	" 3- 7	0.200-0.467
Lithii benzoas,	gr. 2- 5	0.133-0.333
bromid, . .	" 1- 3	0.066-0.200
carb, . . .	" 2- 6	0.133-0.400
citr, . . .	" 2- 5	0.133-0.333
salicylas, .	" 2- 8	0.133-0.533
Lupulinum, .	" 5-10	0.333-0.666
Magnesia, .	" 15-60	1.000-4.000
Magnesii carb.	" 15-60	1.000-4.000
citr. gran.,	ʒ 2- 8	8.000-32.000
sulphas, .	" 2- 8	8.000-32.000
sulphis, . .	gr. 8-30	0.533-2.000
Manganese binox, . .	" 2- 4	0.133-0.266
Mangani sulph	" 2-10	0.133-0.666
Manna, . .	℥ 1- 2	32.000-64.000
Massa copaibæ	gr. 5-30	0.333-2.000
ferri carb, .	" 5-15	0.333 1.000
hydrarg, .	" 1-15	0.066-1.000
Mist. ammon.,	ʒ 4- 8	16.000-32.000
asafœtidæ,	" 4- 8	16.000-32.000
chloroformi,	" 1- 2	4.000-8.000
cretæ, . .	℥ 1- 2	32.000-64.000
ferri comp.,	" ½ - 2	16.000-64.000
ferri et amm. acet., . .	" ½ - 1	16.000-32.000
glycyrrh. comp., .	ʒ 1 4	4.000-16.000
magnes. et asafœt., .	" 1- 4	4.000-16.000
potassii citr.	℥ ½ 2	16.000-64.000
rhei et sodæ,	" ½ 1	16.000-32.000
Morphina and its salts, .	gr. $\frac{1}{16}$-½	0.004-0.033
Moschus, . .	" 2-15	0.133-1.000
Narceina, . .	" $\frac{1}{6}$-½	0.011-0.033
Nitroglycerin. (1 % sol.),	♏ 1	0.033
Nux vomica,	gr. 1- 5	0.066-0.333
Oleoresina aspidii, . .	" 15-60	1.000-4.000
capsici, . .	" $\frac{1}{6}$ ½	0.011-0.033
cubebæ, . .	♏ 5-20	0.333-1.333
filicis, . .	" 30-60	2.000-4.000
lupulini, .	gr. 2- 5	0.133-0.333
piperis, . .	" 1- 3	0.066-0.200
zingiberis, .	" 1- 3	0.066-0.200
Oleum copaibæ	♏ 8-15	0.533-1.000
cubebæ, . .	" 15-30	1.000-2.000
eriger, . .	" 5-15	0.333-1.000
eucalypti, .	" 5-10	0.333-0.666
phosphorat.,	" 1 3	0.066-0.200
sabinæ, . .	" 1 3	0.066-0.200
terebinth, .	" 5-30	0.333-2 000
tiglii, . .	" $\frac{1}{6}$- 1½	0.011-0.100
Opium (14 % morphine)	gr $\frac{1}{6}$- 1½	0.010-0.100
Pepsinum pur.	gr. 15-ʒ ½	1.000-2.000
saccharatum	gr. 30-ʒ 1	2.000-4.000
Phosphorus, .	gr. $\frac{1}{128}$-$\frac{1}{50}$	0.0005-0.0013
Physostigmin. salic, . .	" $\frac{1}{120}$-$\frac{1}{64}$	0.0005-0.001
sulphas, .	" $\frac{1}{128}$-$\frac{1}{64}$	0.0005-0.001
Picrotoxinum.	" $\frac{1}{64}$-$\frac{1}{8}$	0.001-0.008
Pilocarpina, and salts,	" $\frac{1}{64}$-½	0.001-0.033
Pil. aloes, .	Pills 1-3	
aloes et asaf.	" 2-5	
aloes et ferri	" 1-3	

Remedies.	Dose. Apoth.	Dose. Metric.
Pil. aloes et mast, . .	Pills 1-3	
aloes et myrrhæ,	" 2-5	
antim. comp.	" 1-3	
asafœtidæ,	" 1-6	
cathar.comp.	" 1-4	
ferri comp.,	" 2-5	
ferri iodidi,	" 1-4	
galbani comp	" 1-5	
opii, . . .	" 1-2	
phosphori, .	" 1-4	
rhei, . . .	" 2-5	
rhei comp.,	" 2-5	
Piperinum, .	gr. 1 8	0.066-0.533
Plumbi acetas,	" ½ 3	0.033-0.200
iodidum, .	" ½- 3	0.033-0.200
Potassii acetas	" 15-60	1.000-4.000
bicarb, . .	" 8-60	0.533-4.000
bitartr, . .	ʒ 1- 2	4.000-8.000
bromid, . .	gr. 8-60	0.533-4.000
carb, . . .	" 8-30	0.533-2.000
chloras, . .	" 8-30	0.533-2.000
citras, . .	" 15-60	1.000-4.000
cyanid. . .	" $\frac{1}{16}$ ⅛	0.004-0.008
et sodii tartr.	℥ ½- 1	16.000-32.000
hypophosph.	gr. 5-15	0.333-1.000
iodid, . . .	" 2-15	0.133 1.000
nitras, . .	" 8-15	0.533-1.000
sulphas, .	ʒ 1- 4	4.000-16.000
sulphidum,	gr. 1-10	0.066-0.666
sulphis, . .	" 15-30	1.000-2.000
tartras, . .	ʒ 1- 8	4.000-32.000
Pulv. antimon.	gr. 1- 3	0.066-0.200
aromat, . .	" 8 30	0.533-2.000
cretæ comp.,	" 8 30	0.533-2.000
glycyrrh. comp., .	" 30-60	2.000-4.000
ipecac. comp.	" 5-15	0.333-1.000
jalapæ comp.	" 30-60	2.000-4.000
morph. comp	" 8-15	0.533-1.000
rhei comp.,	" 30-60	2.000-4.000
Quinidina, and salts, . .	" 1-30	0.066-2.000
Quinina, and salts, . .	" 1-30	0.066-2.000
Quinin. arsen.	" $\frac{1}{6}$- 1	0.011-0.066
Resina copaib.	" 2 10	0.133-0.666
jalapæ, . .	" 2- 5	0.133-0.333
podophylli,	" ⅛ ½	0.008-0.033
scammonii,	" 2-10	0.133-0 666
Resorcin, . .	" 2- 5	0.133 0.333
Rheum, . .	" 2-30	0.133-2.000
Salicinum, .	" 8-30	0.533-2.000
Salol, . . .	" 10-15	0 666-1.000
Santonica, .	" 8-60	0 533-4.000
Santoninum,	" 1- 5	0.066-0.333
Sapo, . . .	" 5-30	0.333-2.000
Scammonium.	" 3-15	0.200 1.000
Senna, . . .	" 8-60	0.533-4.000
Sodii acetas, .	" 15-60	1.000-4.000
arsenias, .	" $\frac{1}{64}$-$\frac{1}{10}$	0.001-0.006
benzoas, .	" 5-15	0.333-1.000
bicarb, . .	" 8-30	0.533 2.000
bisulphis, .	" 8-30	0.533-2.000
boras, . .	" 8-30	0.533-2.000
bromid, . .	" 8-30	0.533-2.000
carb, . . .	" 8-30	0.533-2.000
carb. exsicc.,	" 5-15	0.333-1.000
chloras, . .	" 5-30	0.333-2.000
hypophosph.	" 8-15	0.533-1.000

Remedies.	Dose. Apoth.	Dose. Metric.
Sodii hyposulp.	gr. 8–30	0.533–2.000
iodidum, .	" 5–15	0.333–1.000
phosphas, .	" 2–15	0.133–1.000
salicylas, .	" 5–30	0.333–2.000
santoninas,	" 2–10	0.133–0.666
sulphas, .	" 1– 2	0.066–0.133
sulphis, . .	" 8–30	0.533–2.000
Spiritus æther. compositus	♏ 30–60	2.000–1.000
æther. nitro.	ʒ ½– 2	2.000–8.000
ammoniæ, .	♏ 8–30	0.533–2.000
ammoniæ arom., .	" 15–60	1.000–4.000
camphoræ,	" 8–30	0.533–2.000
chloroformi,	" 15–60	1.000–1.000
lavend. comp	" 30–60	2.000–1.000
menth. pip.,	" 30–60	2.000–4.000
Strychnina, and salts,	gr. 1/64–1/12	0.001–0.005
Sulphur, . .	ʒ ½– 4	2.000–16.000
Syr. calcii lactophos, .	" 1– 2	4.000–8.000
calcis, . .	♏ 15–30	1.000–2.000
ferri bromidi	" 15–60	1.000–4.000
ferri iodidi,	" 15–40	1.000–2.666
ferri oxidi,	ʒ 1	4.000
ferri hypoph.	" 1	4.000
fer. quin. et str. phos.,	" 1	4.000
hypophosph.	" 1	4.000
hypophosph. c. fer., .	" 1	4.000
ipecac., . .	" ½– 1	2.000–4.000
krameriæ, .	" ½– 4	2.000–16.000
lactucarii, .	" 1– 3	4.000–12.000
rhei, . . .	" 1– 4	4.000–16.000
rhei arom.,	" 1– 4	4.000–16.000
rosæ, . . .	" 1– 2	4.000–8.000
sarsap. comp.	" 1– 4	4.000–16.000
scillæ, . .	" ½– 1	2.000–4.000
scillæ comp.	♏ 15–60	1.000–4.000
senegæ, . .	ʒ 1– 2	4.000–8.000
sennæ, . .	" 1– 4	4.000–16.000
Thalline, . .	gr. 2–15	0.133–1.000
Theine (hypo.)	" 1/6– 1	0.011–0.066
Tinct. aconiti fol., . .	♏ 8–16	0.533–1.000
aconiti rad.,	" 1– 5	0.066–0.333
aconiti rad., Fleming's,	" ⅔– 2	0.044–0.133
aloes (1880),	ʒ ½– 2	2.000–8.000
aloes et myr.	" 1– 2	4.000–8.000
arnicæ flor.,	♏ 8–30	0.533–2.000
arnicæ rad.,	" 15–30	1.000–2.000
assafœtidæ,	" 30–60	2.000–1.000
belladonnæ,	" 8–15	0.533–1.000
bryoniæ, .	" 15–30	1.000–2.000
calendulæ,	" 15–30	1.000–2.000
calumbæ, .	ʒ 1– 4	4.000–16.000
cannab. ind.,	♏ 15–30	1.000–2.000
cantharid, .	" 8–15	0.533–1.000
capsici, . .	" 8–15	0.533–1.000
catech. comp	ʒ ½– 2	2.000–8.000
chirretta, .	♏ 15–60	1.000–4.000
cimicifugæ,	" 30–60	2.000–4.000
cinchonæ, .	ʒ ½– 2	2.000–8.000
cinch. comp.	" ½– 2	2.000–8.000
colchici rad.,	♏ 5–15	0.333–1.000
colchici sem.	" 6–15	0.400–1.000
conii, . .	" 5–30	0.333–2.000
croci, . .	ʒ 1– 2	4.000–8.000

Remedies.	Dose. Apoth.	Dose. Metric.
Tinct. cubebæ,	ʒ 1– 2	4.000–8.000
digitalis, .	♏ 6–15	0.400–1.000
ferri acet., .	" 15–30	1.000–2.000
ferri chloridi	" 15–30	1.000–2.000
ferri chloridi æther, .	" 15–30	1.000–2.000
ferri pomati,	" 20–60	1.333–4.000
gallæ, . .	ʒ ½– 2	2.000–8.000
gelsemii, .	♏ 8–15	0.533–1.000
guaiaci, .	" 30–60	2.000–4.000
guaiaci am.,	" 30–60	2.000–4.000
hellebori, .	" 10–15	0.666–1.000
humuli, .	ʒ 1– 2½	4.000–10.000
hydrastis, .	♏ 30–90	2.000–6.000
hyoscyami fol., . .	" 15–30	1.000–2.000
hyoscy. sem	" 15–30	1.000–2.000
ignatiæ, .	" 5–15	0.333–1.000
iodi, . . .	" 5–15	0.333–1.000
ipecac. et op.	" 5–15	0.333–1.000
jalapæ, . .	ʒ ½– 2	2.000–8.000
kino, . . .	" ½– 2	2.000–8.000
krameriæ, .	" ½– 2	2.000–8.000
lavend comp	" ½– 2	2.000–8.000
lobeliæ, .	♏ 15–45	1.000–3.000
lupulini, .	ʒ ½– 2	2.000–8.000
matico, . .	" ½– 2	2.000–8.000
moschi, . .	♏ 15–60	1.000–4.000
nux vomicæ,	" 8–20	0.533–1.333
opii, . . .	" 8–15	0.533–1.000
opii camp.,	" 8–75	0.533–5.000
phytolaccæ,	" 8–60	0.533–4.000
physostigm.	" 5–15	0.333–1.000
pyrethri, .	" 8–30	0.533–2.000
quassiæ, .	ʒ ½– 2	2.000–8.000
rhei, . . .	" 1– 8	4.000–32.000
rhei arom.,	♏ 30–75	2.000–5.000
rhei dulc., .	ʒ 1– 4	4.000–16.000
sanguinariæ	♏ 15–60	1.000–4.000
scillæ, . .	" 8–60	0.533–4.000
serpentariæ,	ʒ ½– 2	2.000–8.000
stramm. fol.,	♏ 8–15	0.533–1.000
stramm. sem.	" 6–15	0.400–1.000
sumbul, .	" 8–30	0.533–2.000
valer, . .	ʒ ½– 2	2.000–8.000
valer. amm.,	" ½– 2	2.000–8.000
veratr. vir.,	♏ 3–10	0.200–0.666
zingiberis, .	" 15–60	1.000–4.000
Tritur. elater.,	gr. 1/8–½	0.008–0.033
Urethane, .	" 10–15	0.666–1.000
Veratrina, .	" 1/64–1/10	0.001–0.006
Vin. aloes, .	ʒ 1– 2	4.000–8.000
antim. exp. et alt., .	♏ 1– 8	0.066–0.533
emetic, .	" 30–75	2.000–5.000
colch. rad.,	" 8–20	0.533–1.333
colch. sem.,	" 5–30	0.333–2.000
ergotæ, . .	ʒ 1– 3	4.000–12.000
ferri amar.,	" 1	4.000
ferri citrat.,	" 1	4.000
ipecac, exp.,	♏ 5–15	0.333–1.000
emetic, .	ʒ 3– 6	12.000–24.000
opii, . . .	♏ 5–15	0.333–1.000
rhei, . . .	ʒ 1– 2	4.000–8.000
Zinci acet., .	gr. 1– 2	0.066–0.133
bromid, . .	" ½– 2	0.033–0.133
iodid., . .	" ½– 3	0.033–0.200
oxid., . .	" 1–10	0.066–0.666
phosphid., .	" 1/10–1/6	0.006–0.011
sulphas emet	" 15–30	1.000–2.000
valerianas,	" 1– 6	0.066–0.400

A LIST OF NEW REMEDIES,

Prepared Expressly for The Physician's Visiting List for 1892.

ARISTOL.—This is a substance introduced into medicine for the purpose of substituting iodoform. It is a compound of iodine and thymol, containing 45.8 % of iodine. Eichhoff has reached the following conclusions concerning it:—

1. That aristol is in all cases a harmless drug.
2. That it is a powerful parasiticide.
3. That in the ulcerations of tertiary syphilis, curative results are obtained more rapidly than with any other drug.
4. It is the most useful of all applications in the treatment of lupus.
5. In the treatment of psoriasis, it does not act quite as rapidly as chrysarobin or pyrogallic acid.

The aristol was in most cases applied as a ten per cent. ointment in vaseline.

BENZOATE OF BISMUTH.—Benzoate of bismuth has been used by Finger in the local treatment of soft chancre with great success. In each case the surface of the sore was thoroughly washed, and a thin layer of the benzoate applied by means of a soft brush. After this the spot was entirely covered with cotton, which was held in place by an adhesive strip or bandage. The strips should be changed once or twice in twenty-four hours. While at first they may produce slight burning and pricking, no discomfort ensues. The surface of the ulcer rapidly becomes healthy, and the discharge of pus is checked after the third or fourth day, and cicatrization takes place.

BROMIDE OF ETHYL.—Bromide of ethyl has been before the profession for a number of years as an anæsthetic, but has recently been still further tried in Germany. It exercises a greater depressing power over the heart than chloroform, but possesses certain advantages which may be summarized in the following words:—

1. Bromide of ethyl acts with great rapidity, and usually without a period of excitement. It is stated to be perfectly safe when used in small amounts, and there are seldom any unpleasant after-effects.
2. The best method of administration is to pour the entire quantity to be used (1 to 5 drachms) on an impermeable mask, which is placed close to the patient's mouth and nose.
3. In most cases the operation can be begun in from fifteen to twenty seconds after the first inhalation, though the duration of anæsthesia will be very short. Only suitable for minor operations, opening abscesses, etc.
4. There are a few patients, chiefly alcoholics, who cannot be anæsthetized by the agent.
5. There are no contra-indications to the use of bromide of ethyl employed in small amounts and for short operations.

CHLORALAMIDE.—This is a new hypnotic, producing sleep in most cases when administered in ordinary doses, but not so active as chloral or morphia. It is a combination of anhydrous chloral and formamid, and the advantages which are claimed for it consist in its comparatively feeble influence over the circulatory system as compared to its hypnotic power over the brain. It has rather a sharp taste and is fairly soluble in water. The ordinary dose is from 20 to 40 grains, and the sleep which it produces generally lasts from five to eight hours.

CONVALLARIA.—A heart-tonic like digitalis in action, but without the bad effect upon the stomach, etc., and without danger from cumulative action. Dose, of the Extract, gr. xv–xxv.

CREOLIN.—A complex antiseptic and disinfectant, consisting of four groups of compounds—soaps, creolin oil, phenols and pyridines. Several cases of poisoning have been reported from its internal administration.

DIURETIN.—A sodio-salicylic compound of theobromine, alleged to produce the beneficial effects of the same, without the unpleasant symptoms. Dose, grams 6 daily, in one gram doses.

EUPHORINE.—*Phenyl-urethan*, derived from aniline,—a white crystalline powder, insoluble in water, but soluble in weak alcohol. In doses of 15–20 grains in 24 hours, Sansom commends it as an antipyretic, as an anti-rheumatic and analgesic. It seems inferior to other remedies of a similar nature.

EXALGIN—Exalgin or methylacetanilide, has recently come into service both as an antipyretic and analgesic. It resembles antifebrin in many particulars, but has been found more valuable in painful affections than the latter drug. It is valuable in all forms of neuralgia, and is not so apt to produce disagreeable symptoms as antifebrin. The dose is from 4 to 8 grains. Generally it is given in a mixture with alcohol, syrup, or water. Very large doses of it produce darkening of the blood and cause the formation of methæmoglobin. To be used with caution.

GURJUN OIL.—Gurjun balsam, or "wood oil," is a balsamic exudation obtained by incision and the application of heat, from the trunk of an East Indian tree. It is a transparent liquid of the consistence of olive oil, of an opaque, dingy, greenish-gray color as seen by reflected light, and having an aromatic odor and taste not unlike that of copaiba, but without its acridity. It is first to be given in doses of a drachm, and then of two drachms, three times a day, in the form of a mixture with liquor potassæ, spirit of nitrous ether, mucilage of acacia, and cinnamon water. Chronic sufferers from bronchitis, many of whom have previously taken copaiba, report that it acts admirably as an expectorant, "clearing the chest" and easing the cough. In some cases tincture of jaborandi or nitrate of pilocarpine may be added at bedtime, so as to produce profuse sweating. It would seem that gurjun oil has all the advantages of copaiba as an expectorant, without the grave disadvantage of exciting an eruption.

HYPNAL.—*Trichloraldehyd phenyldimethyl pyrazol.* A compound resulting from the combination of chloral hydrate and antipyrin, having the properties of both constituents. Dose gr. j.

METHACETIN.—This is a new antipyretic introduced into medicine within the last year as a substitute for the older drugs. It seems to act with about the same power as does antipyrin, dose for dose, but is by no means so useful in the relief of pain, although it is said to act quite as favorably in rheumatism. The advantages which are claimed for it consist in its freedom from harmful effects, although it is admitted that the sweating which it produces is more profuse. The ordinary dose for an adult is from 3 to 8 grs., according to the height of the temperature.

METHYLAL.—A local anæsthetic and an efficient hypnotic. Dose, ℥iv-v, repeated at short intervals.

METHYL CHLORIDE.—This drug is now coming into use more and more as a local anæsthetic. It is a colorless, easily liquefied gas, with an odor resembling that of ether and chloroform. The readiness with which the gas liquefies adapts it for convenient use, as it can be stored in a siphon or in a bottle. It may be applied to the skin directly from the siphon, or as a spray. Better still, a cotton tampon may be saturated with it, and applied over the area which it is desired to anæsthetize, the cotton being held by means of a wooden handle. After a few moments' contact the skin becomes pale, and the application should be continued a few seconds longer, until the skin becomes perfectly white and parchment-like in appearance. By applying methyl chloride too long, it is possible to produce a local slough. It is useful in minor surgical operations, such as opening boils and abscesses.

MUSSANIN.—This substance has been introduced into medicine as a vermifuge, and is the active principle of the bark of an Abyssinian tree (Acacia Anthelmintica). It is very much more active and powerful in its effects than koosso, and the taste is more agreeable. The powdered bark may be given in the dose of 1 to 2 ounces, or administered in the form of the infusion.

NAPHTHALINE.—A coal tar derivative, with a dosage of gr. li–viij, up to lxxx per diem for adults. From it are derived NAPHTHOL and HYDRONAPHTHOL. All are antiseptic, used as intestinal, vesical and local antiseptics, disinfectants and germicides.

NAREGAMIA.—A useful expectorant, especially when there is an irritative cough due to scanty bronchial secretion, or when the sputum is so tough as to make expectoration difficult. The tincture should not be employed pure, but combined in the proportion of 1 to 8 parts with cherry laurel water. The dose of the tincture is 15 to 30 minims.

OREXIN.—This is a new stomachic, quite soluble in water, but very irritating to all mucous membranes when in concentrated form. It is best administered in the form of the hydrochlorate in the dose of 20 grains, given with extract of gentian in pill form, and immediately followed by a glass of water or cup of broth. In certain cases of lost appetite depending upon gastric depression, orexin is asserted to be of signal success.

PARALDEHYDE.—A polymeric modification of aldehyde, a powerful hypnotic and diuretic, but without diaphoretic action. It possesses many of the qualities of chloral, without its dangers. Dose ♏xx-ʒj.

PEROXIDE OF HYDROGEN.—*Hydrogen dioxide.* A powerful antiseptic that is rapidly growing in favor, because comparatively speaking, harmless, tasteless and odorless, and may be used internally or externally. The 15 volume preparation is most commonly used. Of especial value in infectious diseases of the skin, nose and throat.

PHENACETINE.—A tasteless, white, glossy crystalline powder. An efficient antirheumatic, antipyretic and antineuralgic, with no disagreeable after-affects. Recommended in whooping-cough, dissolved in glycerine. Dose gr. 1 to 20.

PYOKTANIN.—"Pus-killer." A coal-tar derivative, purified methylviolet, is recommended especially by Stilling, as a reliable germicide of especial service in all cases where purulent discharges exist, such as ulcers, etc. The drug is very diffusible, comparatively harmless, the blue variety having an intense but temporary staining power. It is commonly used in solutions of the strength of one to a thousand.

SALICYLATE OF MERCURY.—Salicylate of Mercury has been used very largely recently in the treatment of syphilis by the hypodermic method. It is to be suspended in paraffin oil in the proportion of 22 grains of the salicylate to three drachms of the oil. The bottle containing this mixture must be thoroughly shaken before its contents are used, and the needle should be kept in pure paraffin oil and carefully cleaned before and after the injection. In the beginning of the treatment one minim of this mixture should be injected every fourth day, the injections being sent deeply into the glutei. Remarkable results are claimed for this treatment in cases where the stomach will not stand the administration of drugs.

SOMNAL.—A complex body, formed by the union of chloral, alcohol and urethane. Said to be a more certain hypnotic than urethane, and less depressing than chloral, being without the depressing effect of sulphonal. The dose is from 30 to 140 minims.

SULPHONAL.—An excellent hypnotic, tolerance to which is apt to be established in time, and sometimes having unpleasant after-affects. An odorless, tasteless, white crystalline substance, only slightly soluble in water. Dose gr. xv-xlv.

THYMOL.—A stearoptene, contained in oil of thyme. Dose gr. ss-ij. A powerful antiseptic and disinfectant. It is more powerful than carbolic acid, and much less poisonous.

TRIONAL AND TETRONAL.—Substances allied to sulphonal in constitution, dosage and effects, containing respectively four and three ethyl groups. May be used in those cases proving refractory to sulphonal.

URETHANE.—*Ethyl carbamate.* An hypnotic, not so reliable as paraldehyde or chloral, and with continued use, tolerance seems soon to be established. It produces a refreshing sleep, without bad effects. Dose gr. xv-ʒj, but best given in 5 grain doses, repeated frequently.

INCOMPATIBILITY.

S. O. L. POTTER, A.M., M.D.,

AUTHOR OF "A COMPEND OF MATERIA MEDICA AND THERAPEUTICS," AND OF
"A HANDBOOK OF MATERIA MEDICA, PHARMACY AND THERAPEUTICS."

Incompatibility gives rise to many dangers which may in a great measure be avoided by the use of the utmost simplicity in prescribing. "The tendency of the present age is toward mono- rather than poly-pharmacy, and prescriptions with the orthodox *adjuvans* and *corrigens* are less frequently seen than formerly." (Piffard.)

This subject can only be glanced at here. The following simple rules may help the burdened memory of the practitioner :—

Never use more than one remedy at a time, if one will serve the purpose

Never use strong mineral acids in combination with other agents, unless you know exactly what reaction will ensue. They decompose salts of the weaker acids and form ethers with alcohol.

Select the simplest solvent, diluent, or excipient you know of, remembering that the solvent power of alcohol and water, for their particular substances, decreases in proportion to the quantity of the other added.

Never combine *Free Acids* with hydrates or carbonates.

Generally do not combine two or more soluble salts.

The following more or less insoluble salts will be formed whenever the materials of which they are composed are brought together in solutions; the Hydrates, Carbonates, Phosphates, Borates, Arseniates and Tannates of most earthy and heavy metals and alkaloids, and the metallic Sulphides; the Sulphates of Calcium, of Lead, and of the subsalts of Mercury ; the Chlorides, Iodides, and Bromides of Bismuth, Silver, Lead, and subsalts of Mercury ; the Iodides of Quinine, Morphine and most alkaloids.

Alkalies precipitate the alkaloids and the soluble non-alkaline metallic salts, and (as also metallic Hydrates and Carbonates) neutralize free acids.

Silver Nitrate, *Lead Acetate*, *Corrosive Sublimate*, *Potassium Iodide* should nearly always be prescribed alone. The first with Creasote forms an explosive compound. *Aconite* should never be given in any vehicle except water.

Silver Nitrate, and *Lead Acetate* and *Subacetate*, although incompatible with almost everything, may be combined with Opium : the latter forming with Opium a compound which, although insoluble, is therapeutically active as a lotion.

Corrosive Sublimate is incompatible with almost everything, and should be given in *Simple Syrup* ; even the Compound Syrup of Sarsaparilla is said to decompose it.

Tannic Acid, and substances containing it, are incompatible with albumen and gelatin. *Tannic Acid*, *Iodine*, and the *soluble Iodides* are incompatible with the alkaloids and substances containing them, and with most soluble metallic salts. *Vegetable Infusions* are generally incompatible with metallic salts.

Glucosides, such as Santonin and Colocynthin, should not be prescribed with free acids or Emulsin.

Dangerous Compounds, because poisonous, are : Potassic Iodide with Potassic Chlorate ; Hydrocyanic acid or Potassium Cyanide with metallic Hydrates, Carbonates, Sub-nitrates or Sub-chlorides, as Bismuth Carbonate, or Nitrate, or Calomel.

Explosions would result from the combination of powerful oxidizers with readily oxidizable substances, as—Potassium Chlorate or Permanganate with Tannin, Sugar, Sulphur, Sulphides, Vegetable powders, Glycerin, Alcohol, Tinctures or Ether.

15

POISONS AND ANTIDOTES.

REVISED FOR 1892.

POISON.	ANTIDOTE.
ACIDS, MINERAL	Chalk, magnesia (plaster off wall in emergency), solution carbonate of soda, emollient drinks, fixed oils.
ACONITE	Emetics, stimulants, external and internal, keep up external heat, keep flat on back.
ANTIM. TART.	Vegetable acids, such as *tannic acid*, catechu.
ARSENIC	Freshly precipitated hydrated sesquioxide of iron made by adding magnesia to any iron solution.
ATROPIA	Same as Belladonna.
ARGENTIC NITRATE	Solution of common salt and demulcent drinks. Emetics.
BELLADONNA	Emetics—mustard flour in water; give physostigma or pilocarpine; cold to head.
CANTHARIDES	Emetics, emollient drinks, opiates by mouth and rectum, large draughts of water to flush kidneys.
CARBOLIC ACID	Any soluble sulphate such as magnesia.
CHLORINE WATER	Albumen, white of egg, milk, flour.
CHLOROFORM	Fresh air, artificial respiration (inclining head down, pull tongue forward), brandy and ammonia intravenously in leg, the *hypodermic* injection of 15 ♏ tincture of digitalis and ₁/₆₀ of a grain of atropine.
COLCHICUM	Emetics, followed by demulcent drinks. If *coma* be present, brandy, ammonia, coffee. Opium in large dose. Keep up external heat.
CONIUM	Emetics, followed by stimulants external and internal.
CORROSIVE SUBLIMATE	Albumen, white of egg (4 gr. sublimate require white of one egg), flour, milk. Equal parts of lime water and milk. Emetics, or evacuate stomach by pump.

16

POISON.	ANTIDOTE.
CROTON OIL	Emetics; wash out stomach, followed by mucilaginous fluids, containing opium.
CUPRI SULPH.	Yellow prussiate of potash or soap.
DIGITALIS.	Recumbent posture after emetics. Emetics and opium; give tincture aconite.
ELATERIUM	Demulcent drinks, enemata of opium, and external heat.
HYDROCYANIC ACID	Fresh air and artificial respiration, with cold effusion. Ammonia by inhalation and intravenously in vein of leg.
HYOSCYAMUS	Stomach pump, emetics, stimulants external and internal, physostigma and pilocarpine.
ILLUMINATING GAS	Hypodermatic injections of nitroglycerin are recommended by Kloman, of Baltimore.
IODINE	Emetics and demulcent drinks, starch or flour diffused in water, opium and external heat.
LEAD SALTS	Any soluble sulphate, either magnesia or soda, succeeded by emetics, and afterwards by opium and milk.
LOBELIA	Stimulants externally and internally; external heat.
MORPHINE	Same as Opium.
NUX VOMICA	30 grs. of chloral and 60 grs. of bromide of potash. Nitrite of amyl.
OPIUM	Atropine hypodermatically till respirations number 8 per minute. Stomach pump, stimulants, external and internal, brandy and coffee, cold affusion, ammonia to nostrils, galvanic shocks, compelling to move about, artificial respiration, electric brush.
OXALIC ACID	Lime, not potash or soda.
PHOSPHORUS	Sulphate of copper in emetic dose as chemical antidote. No oils. Emetics, and purgatives.
POTASH AND SODA SALTS	Dilute acetic acid, citric acid, lemon juice, fixed oils, demulcents, vinegar.
STRAMONIUM	Same as Belladonna.
STRYCHNINE	Same as nux vomica.
TOBACCO	Emetic, stimulants external and internal, strychnine, external heat.
ZINC SALTS	Carbonate of soda, emetics, warm demulcent drinks.

17

DISINFECTANTS.

CONDENSED FROM THE CONCLUSIONS OF THE COMMITTEE ON DISINFECTANTS OF THE AMERICAN PUBLIC HEALTH ASSOCIATION.

For Excreta.

(a) In the sick room: For spore-containing material: 1. Chloride of lime in solution, 4 per cent. 2. Mercuric chloride in solution, 1 : 500.[1] In the absence of spores : 3. Carbolic acid in solution, 5 per cent. 4. Sulphate of copper in solution, 5 per cent. 5. Chloride of zinc in solution, 10 per cent.

(b) In privy vaults: Mercuric chloride in solution, 1 : 500.[2]

(c) For the disinfection and deodorization of the surface of masses of organic material in privy vaults, etc.: Chloride of lime in powder.[3]

For Clothing, Bedding, etc.

(a) Soiled underclothing, bed linen, etc.: 1. Destruction by fire, if of little value. 2. Boiling for at least half an hour. 3. Immersion in a solution of mercuric chloride of the strength of 1 : 2000 for four hours.[1] 4 Immersion in a 2 per cent. solution of carbolic acid for four hours.

(b) Outer garments of wool or silk, and similar articles, which would be injured by immersion in boiling water or in a disinfecting solution: 1. Exposure to dry heat at a temperature of 110° C. (230° F.) for two hours. 2. Fumigation with sulphurous acid gas for at least twelve hours, the clothing being freely exposed, and the gas present in the disinfection chamber in the proportion of four volumes per cent.

(c) Mattresses and blankets soiled by the discharges of the sick: 1. Destruction by fire. 2. Exposure to superheated steam—25 pounds pressure—for one hour. (Mattresses to have the cover removed or freely opened.) 3. Immersion in boiling water for one hour. 4. Immersion in the blue solution (mercuric chloride and sulphate of copper), two fluidounces to the gallon of water.

---

[1] A concentrated solution containing four ounces of mercuric chloride and one pound of cupric sulphate to the gallon of water, is recommended as Standard Solution No. 3. Eight ounces of this solution to the gallon of water will give a dilute solution for the disinfection of excreta, containing about 1 : 500 of mercuric chloride, and 1 : 125 of cupric sulphate.

[2] For this purpose the chloride of lime may be diluted with plaster-of-Paris, or with clean, well-dried sand, in the proportion of one part to nine.

[3] The addition of an equal quantity of potassium permanganate as a deodorant, and to give color to the solution, is to be recommended (Standard Solution No. 2).

For the Person.

The hands and general surface of the body of attendants, of the sick, and of convalescents at the time of their discharge from hospital: 1. Solution of chlorinated soda diluted with nine parts of water (1 : 10). 2. Carbolic acid, 2 per cent. solution. 3. Mercuric chloride, 1 : 1000; recommended only for the hands, or for washing away infectious material from a limited area, not as a bath for the entire surface of the body.

For the Dead.

Envelop the body in a sheet thoroughly saturated with : 1. Chloride of lime in solution, 4 per cent. 2. Mercuric chloride in solution, 1 : 500. 3. Carbolic acid in solution, 5 per cent.

For the Sick Room and Hospital Wards.

(a) While occupied, wash all surfaces with: 1. Mercuric chloride in solution, 1 : 1000 (the blue solution containing sulphate of copper may be used). 2. Chloride of lime in solution, 1 per cent. 3. Carbolic acid in solution, 2 per cent.

(b) When vacated : Fumigate with sulphur dioxide for 12 hours, burning 3 pounds of sulphur for every 1000 cubic feet of air space in the room ; then wash all surfaces, including articles of furniture, wood, leather and porcelain, with one of the above-mentioned disinfecting solutions, and afterward with soap and hot water; finally, throw open doors and windows and ventilate freely.

For Merchandise and the Mails.

The disinfection of merchandise and of the mails will only be required under exceptional circumstances; free aeration will usually be sufficient. If disinfection seems necessary, fumigation with sulphur dioxide, as recommended for woolen clothing, etc., will be the only practicable method of accomplishing it. In order to secure penetration of the envelope by the sulphur dioxide, all mail matter should be perforated by a cutting stamp before fumigating.

☞ Rags used for wiping away infectious discharges should be burned at once. When there is an infectious discharge from throat or nose, use, in place of the usual handkerchief, soft cloths that can be immediately destroyed.

☞ A little disinfectant should always be kept standing in sputa-cups, bed-pans, etc., in the sick room. All excrementitious matter should be carried from the room at once, and should not be emptied in the common water-closet. A good plan is to mix it with sawdust and burn, or bury in a trench so situated as not to drain into any source of water supply.

EXAMINATION OF URINE.

Prepared by JUDSON DALAND, M.D.,

Instructor in Clinical Medicine, University of Pennsylvania.

BASED UPON PROF. JAMES TYSON'S "HANDBOOK FOR PRACTICAL EXAMINATION OF URINE," SEVENTH EDITION.

In the examination of urine, the following are the steps found most convenient in actual practice. Observe:—

    I. The quantity passed in twenty-four hours.
    II. Color and transparency.
    III. Odor.
    IV. Reaction.
    V. Specific gravity.
    VI. Presence or absence of sediment, its quantity and character.
    VII. Presence or absence of albumin.
    VIII. Presence or absence of sugar.

HEAT AND ACID TEST.

The best test for determining the presence of albumin in urine is heat corroborated by nitric acid. To apply this test, fill a test-tube one-fourth its depth with *perfectly clear urine*, to which, if it be not distinctly acid in reaction, *a drop or two* of acetic acid is added—only enough to make it clearly acid--and the fluid boiled over a spirit lamp. If an opacity results, the slightest degree of which becomes visible in a clear urine held in a good light, it is due either to *albumin* or *earthy phosphates.* If the latter, it promptly disappears on the addition of a few drops of nitric acid; *if albumin, it is permanent.*

Acetic acid is preferred to nitric for acidulating the urine, because not only is it true that a small quantity of albumin is dissolved by a large amount of nitric acid, but also that if a drop or two of nitric acid be added to a specimen of albuminous urine, so as to render it distinctly acid, it may happen, on boiling, that no precipitate will appear, although much albumin is present. This is because the serum-albumin is converted into acid-albumin or syntonin, which is not coagulated by heat.

THE NITRIC ACID TEST.

This is best applied according to Heller's method. Upon a convenient quantity of pure, colorless nitric acid in a small test-tube, allow to trickle from a pipette, down the side of the inclined glass, an equal amount of clear urine, which will thus overlie the acid. If albumin is present, there appears at the point of contact between the urine and nitric acid a sharp white band or zone, of varying thickness, according to the quantity of albumin present.

Occasionally, a somewhat similar white zone is formed by the action of nitric acid on the mixed urates if present in excess, by which the more insoluble acid urates are thrown down. This zone might be mistaken for that of albumin, but the acid urates begin to appear, not so much at the border, between the urine and acid, as higher up; nor does the zone on its upper surface remain so sharply defined, but, while under examination, is seen to diffuse itself into the urine above. Further, the application of heat causes its immediate disappearance.

Rarely the urine is so concentrated that nitric acid forms crystals of nitrate of urea, which, however, are dissolved by the application of heat.

THE PICRIC ACID TEST.

Into a test-tube, about six inches long, pour a four-inch column of *clear, transparent* urine; then, holding the tube in a slanting position, pour gently an inch of a saturated solution of picric acid on the surface of the urine, where, in consequence of its low specific gravity (1005), it mixes only with the upper layer of the urine.

As far as the yellow color of the picric acid solution extends, the coagulated albumin renders the liquid turbid, contrasting with the transparent urine below. For the action of the test, *there must be an actual mixture*, and not a mere surface contact. When, in consequence of the scantiness of the albumin, the turbidity is very slight, the application of heat to the upper part of the turbid column increases it. Then, if the tube be placed in a stand, the coagulated albumin will gradually subside, and, in the course of an hour or so, forms a delicate, horizontal film at the junction of the colored and unstained stratum of urine. No previous acidulation of the urine is required, as the picric acid accomplishes this, if needed. Urates, peptones and vegetable alkaloids, like quinine, morphine, etc., are precipitated by picric acid from urine containing them, but.it should be remembered that the application of a *moderate* amount of heat will dissolve the ring thus formed.

BY FEHLING'S SOLUTION.

Place a small quantity of Fehling's solution in a test-tube, and dilute it with about four times its bulk of distilled water, and then boil the mixture for a few seconds. If a precipitate occur, the test solution is worthless, and a fresh supply obtained. To the *boiling, diluted, fresh Fehling's solution* add the suspected urine, drop by drop, and if sugar is present, a yellowish or reddish-yellow precipitate, of the suboxide of copper, appears. Whenever Fehling's solution shows the presence of sugar in the urine, this result should be corroborated by the application of the subnitrate of bismuth, or Bötger's test, as follows :—

SUBNITRATE OF BISMUTH TEST.

Add to urine an equal quantity of liquor potassæ or sodæ and a pinch of ordinary subnitrate of bismuth, and boil; when, if sugar is present, the subnitrate is converted into the black metallic bismuth. If the quantity of sugar is small, the bismuth assumes a grayish hue.

Before applying either of the above tests, albumin, if present, should always be removed by the addition of acetic acid, boiling and filtration.

It should be remembered that occasionally uric acid, creatinin, etc., have the power of reducing Fehling's solution, and thus leading us to erroneously believe sugar to be present.

THE PICRIC ACID AND POTASH TEST.

To a fluid-drachm of suspected urine, add 40 minims of a saturated solution of picric acid and half a drachm of liquor of potassæ. Boil this mixture, and, if sugar is present, a dark, mahogany-red color will be produced.

For quantitative work, perhaps the fermentation test can be most easily applied by the physician.

QUANTITATIVE DETERMINATION OF SUGAR BY THE FERMENTATION TEST.

Having taken the specific gravity of the urine, add a piece of compressed yeast about the size of a walnut, then place it in a warm place, about 80–90° F., for three or four hours, or until Fehling's solution shows no sugar. Allow the urine to cool to the original temperature, and again take the specific gravity. Multiply the number of degrees of specific gravity *lost* by .23, and the result is the percentage amount of sugar present

ASPHYXIA AND APNŒA.

(From Potter's Materia Medica.)

FROM DROWNING.—Remove the person from the water as rapidly and gently as possible, turn the face downwards for a moment, and depress the tongue, in order that water, mucus, etc., may be removed from immediately over the entrance of the windpipe. Give the patient plenty of fresh air, fully exposing neck and chest to the breeze, unless inclement. Turn gently on the face, one forearm being under the forehead, and raise the body up that the water may have free discharge from the mouth. Place patient upon the side and apply stimulants (ammonia, etc.) *near* the nostrils; or the cold douche, in order to excite respiration.

The above measures being ineffectual, convey the body to the nearest convenient spot, strip it carefully and dry it, and place it on a warm bed, with head and shoulders slightly raised, and at once employ one of the following methods.

Silvester's Method.—Pull the tongue forward, to prevent obstruction to entrance of air into the windpipe; produce expansion of the chest by drawing the arms from the sides of the body and upwards until they almost meet over the head. Then bring the arms down to the sides again, causing the elbows almost to meet over the pit of the stomach, and thus producing contraction of the chest. This imitation of the act of respiration should be continued at the rate of fifteen or sixteen times a minute, as in health.

Marshall Hall's Method.—The person should be placed flat on the face, gentle intermittent pressure being made with the hands on the back, the body turned on the side, or a little beyond, then on the face, and the same pressure, etc., continued as at first. The whole body must be worked simultaneously. The same number and frequency of these artificial processes of respiration should be employed as in the other method.

The Michigan Method.—Lay the body face down, the head upon the arm, and stand astride it; grasp it then about the shoulders and armpits, and raise the chest as high as you can without lifting the head quite off the arm, and hold it about three seconds; then replace the body upon the ground, and press the lower ribs downwards and upwards, with slowly-increasing force, for ten seconds; then suddenly let go, to perform the lifting process again.

Whichever process be employed, the effort to restore the temperature of the body must be maintained, the body being well rubbed in an upward direction with the hands, with warm flannels, etc.; bottles of hot water, hot bricks, etc., being applied to the stomach, the axillæ, the soles of the feet, etc., stimulants and beef-tea being judiciously administered when restoration is about taking place. The attempts at resuscitation must be persevered in for several hours, if necessary.

Laryngotomy or tracheotomy, with or without catheterization, or forced insufflations of air or oxygen, have proved successful, as also electro-puncture (Garratt).

In artificial inflation, always press the larynx and trachea against the vertebral column, so as to close the œsophagus and thus prevent the air entering the stomach.

22

After Long Submersion is Recovery Possible ?—According to Harley (p. 001), dogs kept uuder water 1½ minutes always died, if water had entered the luugs. If it had not, the trachea being plugged, they survived a submersion of 4 minutes. When persons rise after sinking they usually get some air, and less speedily come into a state from which recovery is impossible. The greatest period between the last inspiration and the stoppage of the heart is 4 minutes. Some think that no recovery has been made after complete cessation of the heart's action. We infer that after complete submersiou for 5 minutes recovery is iuprobable, unless the person had been previously choked, or in a fainting state, so that no water entered the lungs. But in Anderson's case, the patient had been under water at least 15 minutes, aud iu Garratt's the time was variously estimated at from 15 to 60 minutes.

When is a Case Hopeless ?—Harley says (p. 892): "If the eyes arc opeu, the pupils dilated, the conjunctiva insensible, the counteuauce placid, the skin cold, frothy mucus round the nostrils and mouth, no attempt at respiration, and the heart's action inaudible (when the ear is applied to the chest), the case is hopeless."

SIGNS OF DEATH.—The following have been suggested as methods of deciding whether death has occurred :—

(*a.*) Tie a string firmly about the finger. If the end of the finger becomes swollen aud red, life is not extinct.

(*b.*) Insert a bright steel needle iuto the flesh. If it tarnishes by oxidation in the course of half an hour, life may be considered not extinct.

(*c.*) Inject a few drops of Liquor Ammoniæ under the skin. During life a deep red or purple spot is formed.

(*d.*) Moisten the eye with Atropine. During life the pupil will dilate.

(*e.*) Look at a bright light or at the sun, through the fingers held closely side by side. During life the color is pink ; after death a dead white.

(*f.*) After death a dark spot is said to form gradually on the outer side of the white of the eye, from drying of the sclerotic, so that the dark choroid shows through.

(*g.*) Putrefaction is an absolute sign of death. Better delay for it than run auy risk of burying alive.

FROM FOREIGN BODIES IN AIR PASSAGES.—If round and smooth, invert the patient aud strike on the back : laryngotomy : tracheotomy.

OF THE NEW-BORN.—Clean the mucus out of nostrils and throat ; catheterize the trachea, and suck up the mucus. "Marshall Hall's method :" by placing child on abdomen, then bringing into lateral posture, repeating slowly and deliberately. "Schultze's method :" by placing the thumbs upon the anterior surface of thorax, the iudices in the axillæ, and the other fingers along the back, the face of the child beiug from you ; rotate the child, by swinging upwards, so that the inferior extremities turn over towards you. In a moment re-rotate to the original position. Do not support head or legs iu the forward rotation ; their bending upon or towards the abdomen gives a forced expiration.

COMPARISON OF THERMOMETERS

FROM GOULD'S NEW MEDICAL DICTIONARY.

FAHR.	CENT.	REAC.	FAHR.	CENT.	REAC.
212	100	80	76	24.4	19.6
210	98.9	79.1	74	23.3	18.7
208	97.8	78.2	72	22.2	17.8
206	96.7	77.3	70	21.1	16.9
204	95.6	76.4	68	20	16
202	94.4	75.6	66	18.9	15.1
200	93.3	74.7	64	17.8	14.2
198	92.2	73.8	62	16.7	13.3
196	91.1	72.9	60	15.6	12.4
194	90	72	58	14.4	11.6
192	88.9	71.1	56	13.3	10.7
190	87.8	70.2	54	12.2	9.8
188	86.7	69.3	52	11.1	8.9
186	85.6	68.4	50	10	8
184	84.4	67.6	48	8.9	7.1
182	83.3	66.7	46	7.8	6.2
180	82.2	65.8	44	6.7	5.3
178	81.1	64.9	42	5.6	4.4
176	80	64	40	4.4	3.6
174	78.9	63.1	38	3.3	2.7
172	77.8	62.2	36	2.2	1.8
170	76.7	61.3	34	1.1	0.9
168	75.6	60.4	32	0.	0
166	74.4	59.6	30	-1.1	-0.9
164	73.3	58.7	28	-2.2	-1.8
162	72.2	57.8	26	-3.3	-2.7
160	71.1	56.9	24	-4.4	-3.6
158	70	56	22	-5.6	-4.4
156	68.9	55.1	20	-6.7	-5.3
154	67.8	54.2	18	-7.8	-6.2
152	66.7	53.3	16	-8.9	-7.1
150	65.6	52.4	14	-10	-8
148	64.4	51.6	12	-11.1	-8.9
146	63.3	50.7	10	-12.2	-9.8
144	62.2	49.8	8	-13.3	-10.7
142	61.1	48.9	6	-14.4	-11.6
140	60	48	4	-15.6	-12.4
138	58.9	47.1	2	-16.7	-13.3
136	57.8	46.2	0	-17.8	-14.2
134	56.7	45.3	-2	-18.9	-15.1
132	55.6	44.4	-4	-20	-16
130	54.4	43.6	-6	-21.1	-16.9
128	53.3	42.7	-8	-22.2	-17.8
126	52.2	41.8	-10	-23.3	-18.7
124	51.1	40.9	-12	-24.4	-19.6
122	50	40	-14	-25.6	-20.4
120	48.9	39.1	-16	-26.7	-21.3
118	47.8	38.2	-18	-27.8	-22.2
116	46.7	37.3	-20	-28.9	-23.1
114	45.6	36.4	-22	-30	-24
112	44.4	35.6	-24	-31.1	-24.9
110	43.3	34.7	-26	-32.2	-25.8
108	42.2	33.8	-28	-33.3	-26.7
106	41.1	32.9	-30	-34.4	-27.6
104	40	32	-32	-35.6	-28.4
102	38.9	31.1	-34	-36.7	-29.3
100	37.8	30.2	-36	-37.8	-30.2
98	36.7	29.3	-38	-38.9	-31.1
96	35.6	28.4	-40	-40	-32
94	34.4	27.6	-42	-41.1	-32.9
92	33.3	26.7	-44	-42.2	-33.8
90	32.2	25.8	-46	-43.3	-34.7
88	31.1	24.9	-48	-44.4	-35.6
86	30	24	-50	-45.6	-36.4
84	28.9	23.1	-52	-46.7	-37.3
82	27.8	22.2	-54	-47.8	-38.2
80	26.7	21.3	-56	-48.9	-39.1
78	25.6	20.4			

ROBINSON.

The Latin Grammar of Pharmacy and Medicine.

By H. D. ROBINSON, PH.D., Professor of Latin Language and
Literature, University of Kansas, Lawrence. With an Intro-
duction by L. E. SAYRE, PH.G., Professor of Pharmacy, and
Dean of the Dept. of Pharmacy, in the University of Kansas.
12mo.   275 Pages.   Cloth, $2.00

*** This book is the outgrowth of experience.   It has been de-
signed to meet the wants of pharmaceutical and medical students
whose knowledge of Latin is deficient.   There is no doubt but
that the student whose previous Latin education has been neglec-
ted is at a great disadvantage, compared with those who have
acquired a fair knowledge of that language.   He is much slower
in understanding the terminology of the words used in medicine
and pharmacy, and without a clear knowledge of terms satis-
factory progress is impossible.

By the aid of this book the student is at once introduced to the
Latin that he is brought in contact with, with the words, and
their meanings, that he must use, and the proper prefixes, affixes,
etc., that are so numerous in materia medica and botany.   The
aim has been to make it practical in each detail; the exercises,
questions, etc., relate to the preparing and compounding of medi
cines.

At the end of the work extensive vocabularies—Latin-English
and English-Latin—have been added.

" It is a work that meets with my hearty approval.   There is great need
of just such a book in our American schools of pharmacy and medicine."—
*E. S. Bastin, Professor of Botany, Dept. of Pharmacy, Northwestern
University, Chicago.*

" The object of this useful book is a very laudable one, namely, to improve, if possible, the Latin used by both physicians and druggists, chiefly
in the prescribing of drugs.   While it is true that many of the profession find
it unnecessary to remember the genitive endings of words used in medicine,
because of the customary abbreviations in prescription-writing, there are
others who frequently desire to write their directions to the druggist in
Latin, in order that the patient may not learn of facts about which it is
often necessary for him to remain in ignorance.   We hope that the book
will prove a success, and by its general employment in both pharmaceutical and medical schools, improve the knowledge of Latin in both profes-
sions."—*The Medical News, Philadelphia.*

" It is practical; its arrangement shows the careful and thoughtful genius
of its author, who seems to have comprehended just the need of the student,
and put it in such genial form as to lead the pupil rapidly to an understanding
of what he had feared would be uninteresting and tedious."—*Pharmaceutical Record.*

" I have carefully looked over this work, and I must say I consider it an
exceedingly useful one."—*Prof. H. H. Rusby, College of Pharmacy, City
of New York.*

CHEMICAL BOOKS FOR DRUGGISTS.

Bartley's Medical Chemistry.

Second Edition, Revised. 60 Illustrations.

A Text-Book for Medical and Pharmaceutical Students. By E. H. BARTLEY, M. D., Professor of Chemistry and Toxicology at the Long Island College Hospital; President of the American Society of Public Analysts; Chief Chemist, Board of Health, of Brooklyn, N. Y. Revised and enlarged. With 62 Illustrations. Glossary and Complete Index. 423 pages. 12mo. Cloth, $2.50

*** This book has been prepared expressly for students of Pharmacy and Medicine, and on that account more nearly meets the needs of the average student and is just such a handbook as to be invaluable in the drug store.

"Of this work it may be said that it is condensed without being abrupt, it is detailed without verbosity, and all the instructions are given clearly and distinctly. The oldest and most accomplished physician will be well repaid in having it for a book of reference, while the student will find that it will lighten the burden which, of necessity, he is compelled to carry. It is completed by an excellent set of tables and an index."—*Louisville Medical News.*

Woody's Essentials of Medical Chemistry.

Third Edition. 62 Illustrations.

Essentials of Chemistry and Urinalysis. By SAM E. WOODY, A. M., M. D., Professor of Chemistry and Public Hygiene, and Clinical Lecturer on Diseases of Children, in the Kentucky School of Medicine. Third Edition. 62 Illustrations. 12mo. Cloth, $1.25

"Dr. Woody writes this book, not so much from the standpoint of an original chemist as from that of a teacher, and, knowing the needs of the medical student—as to what he should learn, etc , in medical chemistry—the foundation steps of chemical knowledge are well laid, but in reference to articles, compounds, etc , a careful selection has been made, so as to teach the medical student what he should know about chemistry, while those matters that simply interest the laboratory chemist, without distinct bearing on a pharmacal or medical subject, are omitted. The section on urinalysis is very valuable, and should be mastered by students and practitioners. It is a very valuable book for the practitioner who wishes to know facts without the tedium of giving chemical theories, etc."—*Virginia Medical Monthly,* November, 1890.

BLOXAM'S Text-Book, Inorganic and Organic. Seventh Edition. Cloth, $4.50; Leather, $5.50.

HOLLAND. The Urine, the Poisons and the Milk. Fourth Edition. Cloth, $1.00

RICHTER'S Inorganic Chemistry. A complete Text-Book. Illustrated. Third Edition. 12mo. Cloth, $2.00

RICHTER'S Organic Chemistry. Second Edition. Enlarged and improved. Just ready. Cloth, $4.50

CHEMICAL BOOKS for DRUGGISTS.

Müter. Practical and Analytical Chemistry.

By JOHN MÜTER, F. R. S., F. C. S., etc. Fourth Edition. Revised to meet the requirements of American Medical and Pharmaceutical Colleges by CLAUDE C. HAMILTON, M.D., Professor of Analytical Chemistry in University Medical College and in Kansas City College of Pharmacy, with 51 Illustrations. Octavo. Cloth, $2.00

** The following description gives the chief points added by the American editor:—

Cuts have been added illustrating the process of decantation, use of the blowpipe, the Bunsen burner, taking specific gravity, and analysis of urinary sediments.

The name of each reagent has been inserted where its formula occurs for the first time.

The processes for separating acids or their radicals are collected under one heading to make them apply to detection of impurities, etc.

A table will be found on p. 61 which will enable the student to find readily the pages required for analysis of unknown salts.

Tests for some glucosides, resins, and other organic bodies have been inserted, such as alcohol, chloroform, glycerine, paraldehyde, acetanilide, adeps, lard, aloin chloral hydrate, chrysarobin, elaterin, gelatine, saccharine, iodoform, jalapin, phenacetin, antipyrin, picrotoxin, podophyllin, resorcin, resin, santonin, sulfonal, etc.

The chapter of alkaloids has been enlarged.

Under chapter on volumetric analysis directions are given when to use the different indicators, volumetric solution of potassium permanganate, and estimation of chloral hydrate added, and the standards of strength of each preparation altered to correspond to the U. S. P.

The U. S. P. process for estimating phosphoric acid in the official and dilute acids has also been inserted.

The estimation of fat in milk has been enlarged by addition of the process of exhausting with benzine and decanting.

The U. S. P. process for assaying cinchona, opium, scale preparations, resinous drugs, etc., appears, also, for estimating water in carbolic acid.

The chapter on urine analysis has been extended to twice the space in the English edition, cuts of microscopic sediments added as well as tests for indican, mucin, quantitative estimation of albumen, sugar, and a new scheme for analysis of urinal calculi and form of recording urine analysis.

SUTTON'S Volumetric Analysis. A systematic Handbook. Sixth Edition. Octavo. Cloth, $5.co

TRIMBLE'S Practical and Analytical Chemistry (*the Text-Book at Philadelphia College of Pharmacy*). Third Edition. Illustrated. Octavo. Cloth, $1.50

TYSON. Guide to the Practical Examination of Urine. Seventh Edition, thoroughly revised. Illustrated. Cloth $1.5c

PHARMACY IN A NUTSHELL.

STEWART'S

COMPEND OF PHARMACY.

THIRD REVISED EDITION.

BASED UPON REMINGTON'S TEXT-BOOK

By special permission of Prof. Remington.

BY F. E. STEWART, M.D., PH.G.,

Late Quiz-Master in Chemistry and Theoretical Pharmacy, Philadelphia College of Pharmacy; Demonstrator of Materia Medica and Pharmacy in Jefferson Medical College, etc. With complete tables for conversion of metric to English weights and measures, and the reverse. 12mo.

Strongly bound in cloth. $1.00
Interleaved for the addition of notes, $1.25

*** This book has been prepared to meet the wants of Pharmaceutical students particularly, and the rapid exhaustion of several large editions is ample proof that the author has succeeded in making a book that the student can use to advantage. Each step in the study of Pharmacy is taken up in a systematic, concise manner. All the facts of the science are presented in such a way that they may be easily comprehended and memorized. Any one familiar with the contents of this book need not fear the examinations of any STATE BOARD or COLLEGES OF PHARMACY. It contains a description of each chemical in the U. S. Pharmacopœia, with methods of manufacture, symbolic formulæ, and equations expressing the reactions.

The tables for the conversion of Metric to English weights and measures will prove specially useful, as the new U. S. P. will use the Metric System

The American Journal of Pharmacy says:—

"The work being based upon Prof. Remington's valuable Text-Book of Pharmacy, it does not seem necessary to speak of its scope, arrangement, and general correctness. The facts are well presented and concisely stated, and the book is well adapted for a students' note book, to be used for the thorough study of the subject."

THE BEST STUDENTS' COMPENDS.

MATERIA MEDICA, THERAPEUTICS AND PRESCRIPTION WRITING.
Fifth Revised Edition.

Compend for students, including many unofficial remedies, and with special reference to the Physiological Action of Drugs.

By SAM'L O. L. POTTER, M.A., M.D., F.R.C.P. (Lond.), late A. A. Surgeon, U. S. Army; Professor of the Practice of Medicine, Cooper Medical College, San Francisco. 12mo.

Strongly bound in cloth, $1.00. Interleaved for taking notes, $1.25.

*** Dr. Potter is, without doubt, the most popular writer of students' books. His large experience and his peculiar ability for arranging material in the most attractive manner, without omitting the least matter of importance, has made this the standard Compend. The new edition has been thoroughly revised. Its great value lies in its clearness and conciseness. There is a special section on prescription writing and a list of new remedies. By the use of this book any student can at once familiarize himself with the source, composition, preparation, doses, physiological action, therapeutics, etc., of all the innumerable drugs, both officinal and unofficinal. **Following the description of each drug, there is a list of diseases in the treatment of which it is particularly indicated.**

From J. S. B. Alleyne, M.D., Dean of the Faculty and Professor of Therapeutics and Materia Medica, St. Louis Medical College.
"I find it an admirable digest of the works referred to in the preface, and as such a great aid to the student and practitioner."

MEDICAL CHEMISTRY. Third Edition.

A Compend of Medical Chemistry. Inorganic and Organic. Including Urine Analysis. Chemistry of Tissues and Secretions, Table of Symbols, Valencies and Atomic Weights, etc.

By HENRY LEFFMANN, M.D.,

Professor of Chemistry in the Penn. Col. of Dental Surgery, in the Woman's Medical Col., and in the Philadelphia Polyclinic.

Strongly bound in cloth. $1.00. Interleaved for the addition of notes, $1.25.

*** In preparing his third edition, Dr. Leffmann has included all material that will be found useful to students. It is very much improved. The general principles of chemistry, nomenclature, and points of this kind that must be committed to memory are plainly and clearly stated.

From The Philadelphia Medical and Surgical Reporter.
"What he tells about it he tells in an unusually lucid manner, and he probably tells enough to carry the student through his examination *cura honore.*"

☞ Send for a special illustrated circular of " Blakiston's ? Quiz-Compend? Series." The best Students' Books

VALUABLE REFERENCE BOOKS.

BEASLEY'S Book of Prescriptions. Containing over 3100 Prescriptions, collected from the Practice of the most Eminent Physicians and Surgeons—English, French, and American; a Compendious History of the Materia Medica, Lists of the Doses of all Officinal and Established Preparations, and an Index of Diseases and their Remedies. By HENRY BEASLEY. Seventh Edition. *In press; nearly ready.*

Druggists' General Receipt Book. Comprising a copious Veterinary Formulary; Recipes in Patent and Proprietary Medicines, Druggists' Nostrums, etc.; Perfumery and Cosmetics; Beverages, Dietetic Articles and Condiments; Trade Chemicals, Scientific Processes, and an Appendix of Useful Tables. Ninth Edition. Revised. Cloth, $2.25

Pocket Formulary and Synopsis of the British and Foreign Pharmacopœias. Comprising Standard and Approved Formulæ for the Preparations and Compounds Employed in Medical Practice. Eleventh Edition. Cloth, $2.25

MERRELL'S Digest of Materia Medica. Forming a Complete Pharmacopœia for the use of Physicians, Pharmacists, and Students. By ALBERT MERRELL, M. D. Octavo. Half dark Calf, $4.00

TUSON. Veterinary Pharmacopœia. Including the Outlines of Veterinary Materia Medica and Therapeutics. By R. V. TUSON, F.C.S. Third Edition. 12mo. Cloth, $2.50

MACKENZIE (Sir Morell, M. D.). The Pharmacopœia of the Hospital for Diseases of the Throat and Nose. Fourth Edition, Enlarged, Containing 250 Formulæ, with Directions for their Preparation and Use. 16mo. Cloth, $1.25

PROCTER'S Practical Pharmacy. 43 Engravings and 32 Lithographic Fac-simile Prescriptions. By BARNARD S. PROCTER. Second Edition. Cloth, $4.50.

MUSKETT. Prescribing and Treatment in the Diseases of Children. 32mo. Cloth, $1.75

BALLOU. Veterinary Anatomy and Physiology. By WM. R. BALLOU, M.D., Prof. of Equine Anatomy, New York College of Veterinary Surgeons, Physician to Bellevue Dispensary. 29 Graphic Illustrations. 12mo. Cloth, $1.00

WYTHE. The Physician's Dose and Symptom Book. Containing the Doses and Uses of all the Principal Articles of the Materia Medica, and Officinal Preparations. By JOSEPH H. WYTHE, A.M., M.D. 17th Edition.
Cloth, $1.00; Leather, with Tucks and Pocket, $1.25

VALUABLE REFERENCE BOOKS.

GARDNER. The Brewer, Distiller, and Wine Manufacturer. A Handbook for all interested in the Manufacture and Trade of Alcohol and its Compounds. Illustrated. Cloth, $1.75

Bleaching, Dyeing, and Calico Printing. With Formulæ. Illustrated. $1.75

Acetic Acid, Vinegar, Ammonia, and Alum. Illustrated. Cloth, $1.75

CAMERON. Oils and Varnishes. A Practical Handbook. With Illustrations, Formulæ, Tables, etc. 12mo. Cloth, $2 50

Soap and Candles. A New Handbook for Manufacturers, Chemists, Analysts, etc. Compiled from all reliable and recent sources. 54 Illustrations. 12mo. Cloth, $2.25

TANNER'S Memoranda of Poisons and their Antidotes and Tests. By THOS. HAWKES TANNER, M. D. Sixth American, from the last London Edition. Revised by HENRY LEFFMANN, M. D., Professor of Chemistry in Pennsylvania College of Dental Surgery and in the Philadelphia Polyclinic. 12mo. Cloth, .75

BEALE. On Slight Ailments; their Nature and Treatment. By LIONEL S. BEALE, M.D., F.R.S., Professor of Practice, King's Medical College, London. Second Edition. Enlarged and Illustrated. 8vo. Cloth, $1.25

FENNER'S FORMULARY.

SEVENTH EDITION—OCTAVO.

Containing working Formulas for all official and unofficial preparations used in the Practice of Pharmacy, and the business of the Chemist, Manufacturing Pharmacist, Manufacturer of Proprietary Medicines, Perfumes, etc., etc.

4547 FORMULAS.

1285 PAGES.

OUR PRICE $6.50. USUALLY SOLD FOR $10.00.

☞ Sent, postpaid, to any address upon receipt of $6.50. Orders must come direct to P. Blakiston, Son & Co., Philadelphia.

NOTICE TO DRUGGISTS.

P. Blakiston, Son & Co., 1012 Walnut Street, Philadelphia, deal exclusively in books on

MEDICINE,	**PHARMACY,**
CHEMISTRY,	**DENTISTRY,**
HYGIENE,	**NURSING,**

VETERINARY MEDICINE,

AND THE COLLATERAL SCIENCES.

Catalogues of books on any or all these subjects will be sent free upon application. Correspondence invited.

We keep on hand the **DISPENSATORIES** and **PHARMACOPŒIAS,** and all other books used by the Pharmacist and Student.

We will send any book, postage or express charges prepaid, upon receipt of catalogue price.

** See bottom of page 31 for our price for Fenner's Formulary.

A NEW
MEDICAL DICTIONARY,

INCLUDING ALL THE WORDS AND PHRASES GENERALLY USED IN MEDICINE, WITH THEIR PROPER PRO-NUNCIATION AND DEFINITIONS.

BASED ON RECENT MEDICAL LITERATURE.

BY GEORGE M. GOULD, B.A., M.D.,

Ophthalmic Surgeon to the Philadelphia Hospital and Clinical Chief Ophthalmological Department, German Hospital, Phila-delphia; Editor of " The Medical News."

WITH ELABORATE TABLES OF THE BACILLI, MICROCOCCI, LEUCOMAINES, PTO-MAINES, ETC.; OF THE ARTERIES, GANGLIA, MUSCLES, NERVES AND PLEXUSES; OF WEIGHTS AND MEASURES, THERMOMETERS, ETC.; AND APPENDICES CONTAINING CLASSIFIED TABLES, WITH ANALYSES, OF THE WATERS OF THE MINERAL SPRINGS OF THE U. S., AND TABLES OF VITAL STATISTICS.

☞ Of special use in the Drug Store, as it contains much information about New Remedies and Unofficial preparations not found in any other one book.

www.ingramcontent.com/pod-product-compliance
Lightning Source LLC
Chambersburg PA
CBHW021605270326
41931CB00009B/1370